Stoke-on-Trent

A Journey Through the Potteries

The publishers would like to thank the following companies for their

support in the production of this book

Main sponsor
Goodwin PLC

Bailey Wain & Curzon

R.G. Bassett

James T Blakeman

Clement McGough & Sons

G.C. Dewey

The Diamond Tile Co Ltd

Ferro (Great Britain) Ltd

Gardners Garden Centre

Goodwin Jewellers

Hanley Economic Building Society

E.A Heath (R&W) Ltd

J & R Hill

Johnson Tiles

Keeling & Walker Ltd

S. Keeling & Co.

Moorcroft

Portmeirion

Rafferty Steeplejacks

Spode

Steelite International

Walkers Nonsuch

First published in Great Britain by True North Books Limited
England HX3 6SN
01422 244555

ISBN 978 - 1906649623

Text, design and origination by True North Books

www.truenorthbooks.com

Stoke-on-Trent
A Journey Through the Potteries

CONTENTS

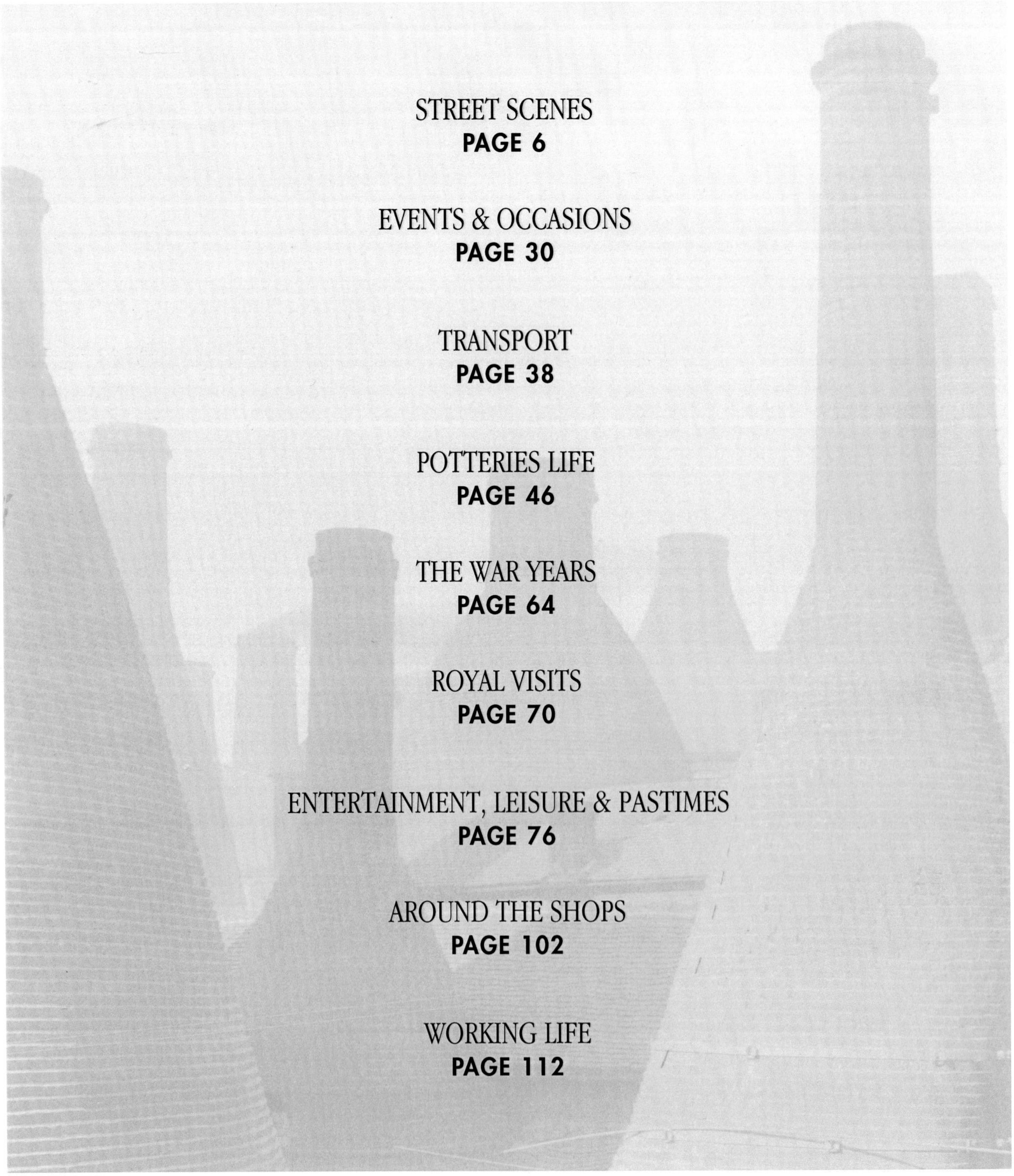

STREET SCENES
PAGE 6

EVENTS & OCCASIONS
PAGE 30

TRANSPORT
PAGE 38

POTTERIES LIFE
PAGE 46

THE WAR YEARS
PAGE 64

ROYAL VISITS
PAGE 70

ENTERTAINMENT, LEISURE & PASTIMES
PAGE 76

AROUND THE SHOPS
PAGE 102

WORKING LIFE
PAGE 112

INTRODUCTION

Such has been the popularity of our previous two books on Stoke and the Potteries area, that we have been encouraged to produce a third publication. The compilation of 'Stoke on Trent – A journey through the Potteries', includes within these pages, even more interesting and thought provoking images from a bygone age. As well as the inclusion of photographs from the 'six towns' that make up Stoke-on-Trent, we are pleased to be able to add a selection of images from Newcastle-under-Lyme and cover the area which forms the Potteries Urban Area.

The history of the area is well documented and because of the uniqueness of several towns being amalgamated together and the stubbornness of Newcastle not to join in the fun, makes it all the more interesting to look back on. Our books allow readers to walk on cobbled streets, browse in well known local shops of the period and revisit special events and occasions, without leaving the comfort of their favourite armchair.

'Change' is relentless and in some parts of the area the transformation will be more obvious than others. The photographs and captions on the pages in this publication serve to remind us of a mere selection of them. Some of the images will be outside 'living memory', however they will be familiar to us, either because they concern an event described to us by a close relative or they feature significant landmarks such as monuments, bridges or buildings. Whatever the view taken on the boundaries which separate 'history', 'nostalgia' or 'the present', we should all invest a little time occasionally to reflect on the past and the people and events which helped to shape life as we know it today.

The companies and organizations which have developed and thrived in the area, over the recent decades, are many. The area has a proud tradition of creativity, enterprise and innovation and we take great pleasure in including in this book histories of an outstanding selection of different companies, whose contribution to the development and sustainability of the city's economic prosperity is a matter of record. With their co-operation and access to their respective photographic archives, we have been able to tell their stories. Hopefully this will trigger the memories of local people who have worked for them, or been touched by their part in community life.

Maybe some readers will spot themselves or a relation, or even a face that you cannot put a name to. In any event we hope you will derive some pleasure from seeing unique images of sights and places you had thought lost forever.... Happy memories!

TEXT	STEVE AINSWORTH, TONY LAX
PHOTOGRAPH COMPILATION	TONY LAX
DESIGNER	SEAMUS MOLLOY
BUSINESS DEVELOPMENT EDITOR	PETER PREST

STREET SCENES

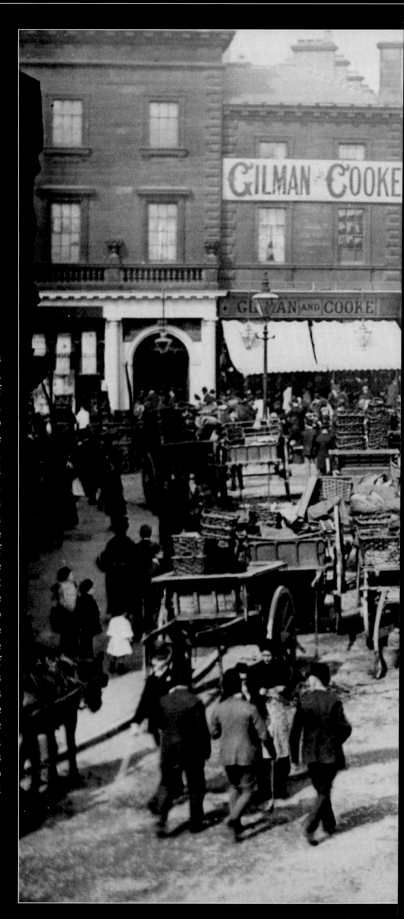

One of the oldest photographs in this book is this one taken in 1880 of Market Square, Hanley. Goods were sold from the back of horse-drawn carts. Market Square was often full as this chaotic scene demonstrates. Traders who arrived late set up stall in Upper Market Square at the junction with Market Street (Parliament Row). Messrs. Gilman and Cooke, Clothiers and Outfitters occupied the corner shop on Market Square and the High Street. In a publication of 1893 Gilman and Cooke was given an outstanding write up: "In a district like that which surrounds Hanley, there are naturally many diverse classes to be catered for, and through the operations of the firm Messrs. Gilman and Cooke, both the middle and working class population have an opportunity that might otherwise be lacking.... "Being a corner shop the establishment possesses the advantage of frontage to the High Street as well as to Market Square.... The premises is in the very heart of the town and the centre of its commercial life..." The building to the right of Gilman & Cooke's would become famous as Swinertons Café. Amies shop sold 'Society Boots'. Next door was Williams & Bedworth, auctioneers. By 1912 the auctioneers building had been turned into The Lyric Electric Theatre - showing silent films. The cinema closed in 1930. At the bottom of Market Square was Pidduck & Sons - famous Hanley jewellers. Their shop first opened in 1841, was refurbished in the 1920s and rebuilt in the 1980s.

Above: This is a picture of Victoria Square, Fenton, from around 1915. On the left are the houses built by local benefactor. William Baker, with the public urinal in front. The pottery works on the right was established in 1825 by the Mason brothers for the manufacture of their famous Ironstone China. In the centre of the picture is a drinking fountain donated by William Baker. The Baker family were known as "the family who built Fenton". William Baker's father (also named William Baker d.1833) was an architect from Audlum, Staffordshire. He bought the estate and manor of Fenton Culvert together with a pottery factory - this was run by his second son (also named William). In 1840, Baker became the first chief bailiff of Fenton, his benefactions included an infant school, Fenton Athenaeum, and the vicarage. He also enlarged the original Christ Church. The drinking water fountain in the centre of the picture originally stood in the Square near Baker's pottery factory opposite Mason's Ironstone works. It was moved to Fenton park to make way for the roundabout and road widening and was subsequently refurbished and in early 2007 moved back to City Road near to the site of the Baker pottery works. Tramlines that can be seen in the foreground were still being removed from Victoria Road more than 30 years after they had last been used by trams in 1928.

Left: Longton has certainly changed a great deal over the last 100 years. This photograph captures the scene in Wharf Street as long ago as 1905. The children in the picture are waiting in the hope of being able to pick up the odd lump of coal falling from coal merchants' carts. For those children whose fathers were in work this was a fine opportunity to make a few extra pennies to spend on sweets. For those whose fathers were unemployed it was a valuable contribution to the household economy when all domestic heating and cooking was reliant upon coal. A generation later it was not only children but grown men who were reduced to scavenging. And not just in the vicinity of coal merchants, mass unemployment and the consequent poverty saw gangs of men scouring railway embankments and colliery spoil heaps for coal in a desperate attempt to keep the home fires burning. Children could make an important contribution to the household budget. Lucky ones could get a paper round. Empty bottles could be returned to the shop for the deposit paid on them. Anyone fortunate enough to find a nearby deposit of sand could excavate it and sell it to shopkeepers to scatter on their floors. But for hard cash coal beat all.

Above: It's quarter to ten in the morning here in Tunstall. And all is well with the world. And these folk would know. In 1900 when this photograph was taken we still owned most of the world. Well if not quite most of it at least enough to be able to say without exaggeration that 'the Sun never sets on the British Empire'. In 1900 Queen Victoria still reigned as she had done since her coronation in the 1830s. Almost certainly no one in this scene has ever known another monarch. They have grown up seeing Victoria's face every day on their coins. The clock tower was new when this photograph was taken. It was erected in 1893, in honour of a local benefactor, Sir Smith Child (1808-1896). Smith Child married Sarah Hill in 1835 and in 1841 moved from Newfield Hall, in Tunstall, to Rownall Hall, in Wetley. He became Conservative MP for North Staffordshire in 1851. On the death of his father-in-law, Smith Child inherited Stallington Hall. He was created a baronet in 1868. A benefactor for several local causes, including colliery disaster funds at Talke in 1868 and at Leycett in 1880, he founded the North Staffordshire Incurables Fund in 1875. He also endowed the Smith Child ward at the North Staffordshire Infirmary.

Above: Here's Snow Hill, Shelton as it was in 1905. Not only does the scene feature the what was then the very latest in public transport, the tram, but also one of the oldest, plain old horseback. The Bell and Bear Inn was built in the mock-tudor style. The building is just the most recent to have occupied the site. The main Hanley road originally ran to the side of the building, that part being known as Cleveland Place. The road continued around the back to emerge between Swynnerton's corner shop and Shelton Church. The earlier Bell and Bear faced the old road, but when the road became a Turnpike, the building was demolished and rebuilt in the tudor-style facing the now re-aligned road known as Snow Hill. The old road was now renamed Cutts Street. The present building dates from 1902, and what looks at first glance like a very old construction was in fact just three years old when this photo was taken. St. Mark's church stands on a prominent site in Shelton; its 120 foot tower is a landmark for miles around. Designed to hold a congregation of 2,100 it is the largest church in the city, measuring 151 feet by 75 feet. It was completed in 1833 in the Early English style at a cost of £10,000. Most of the money came from the Church Commissioners, whose national brief was to finance new centres of Church of England worship in the rapidly expanding areas of population, and Shelton was one of these.

Top right and right: Two views of High Street, Goldenhill, taken some sixty years apart. The first photograph was taken in 1910. It shows a very different High Street to the one pictured in the late 1960s when the trams, their tracks and overhead cables were long gone. And so are the enormous telegraph poles. Much else is gone too. Extensive redevelopment took place in the late 1960s in and around the High Street area of Goldenhill - the main street was widened which resulted in many properties being demolished or losing part of their frontage. Others were improved and a shopping area was developed - many of the photos of Goldenhill from the period were taken as a result of the compulsory purchase order and a Public Enquiry in 1967. The highest point in Stoke-on-Trent the name Goldenhill means "the hill of gold", from the Old English word 'golde'. It may mean the hill where buttercups grow. Goldenhill's development was largely due to the Industrial Revolution. It was situated on the main road to Manchester and Newcastle-under-Lyme, which was turnpiked in 1763. To the west the Trent and Mersey Canal passed Goldenhill, facilitating the transport of both natural and manufactured products in and out of the Potteries. The building of the Harecastle tunnel led to the discovery of coal in the area. James Brindley, the canal engineer, built a branch canal connecting the tunnel to an underground wharf at Goldenhill where he had a share in the

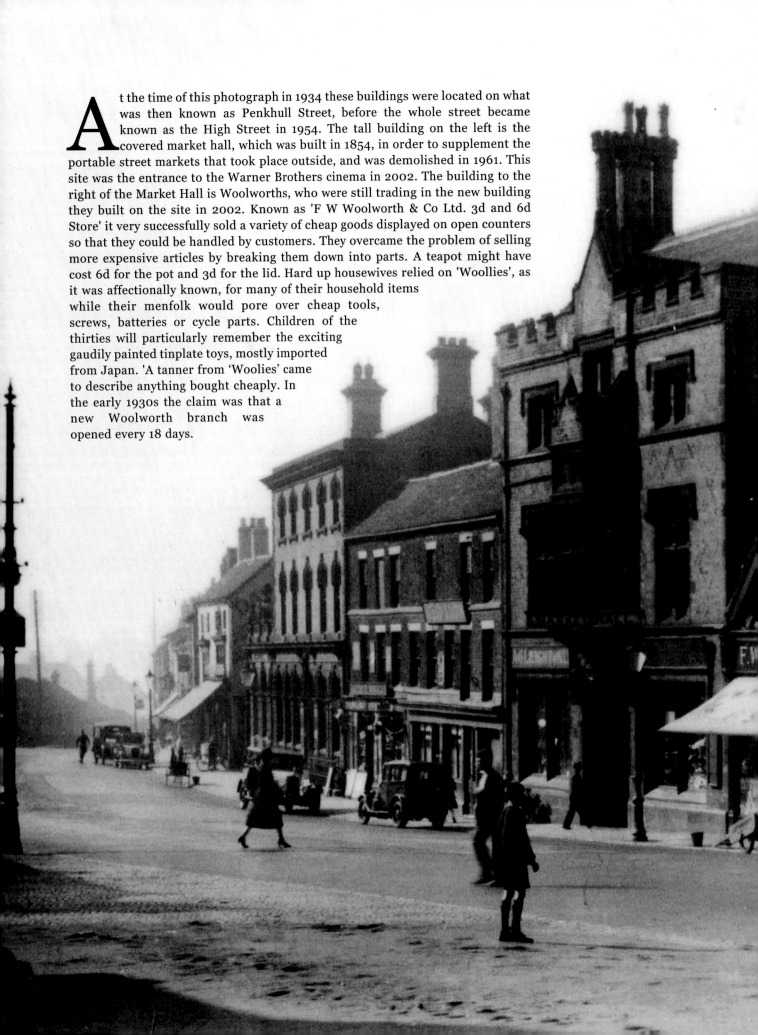

At the time of this photograph in 1934 these buildings were located on what was then known as Penkhull Street, before the whole street became known as the High Street in 1954. The tall building on the left is the covered market hall, which was built in 1854, in order to supplement the portable street markets that took place outside, and was demolished in 1961. This site was the entrance to the Warner Brothers cinema in 2002. The building to the right of the Market Hall is Woolworths, who were still trading in the new building they built on the site in 2002. Known as 'F W Woolworth & Co Ltd. 3d and 6d Store' it very successfully sold a variety of cheap goods displayed on open counters so that they could be handled by customers. They overcame the problem of selling more expensive articles by breaking them down into parts. A teapot might have cost 6d for the pot and 3d for the lid. Hard up housewives relied on 'Woollies', as it was affectionally known, for many of their household items while their menfolk would pore over cheap tools, screws, batteries or cycle parts. Children of the thirties will particularly remember the exciting gaudily painted tinplate toys, mostly imported from Japan. 'A tanner from 'Woolies' came to describe anything bought cheaply. In the early 1930s the claim was that a new Woolworth branch was opened every 18 days.

Crown Bank, Hanley, was a very different place in the first decade of the 20th century from the scene there today. Not many horses around now, that's for sure. And rather more motor cars and fewer pedestrians. Crown Bank is an open area adjacent to Stafford Street, immediately beyond is Piccadilly. Straight ahead is Fountain Square, right is Market Lane, and behind the photographer is Percy Street. This area was the central point in Hanley for getting a horse drawn cab. In the centre of this scene is a small green roofed building - the cab drivers' shelter which was demolished in 1907. Just out of sight on the photographer's right is the Dolphin public house. The Midland Bank would subsequently occupy the same spot. The white building on the right of the picture is Millers House Furnishers and Haberdashers established in 1840. The horse in the foreground is happily having a break, and enjoying snack from its nose bag.

Top right, facing page: Electric street lights, town gas and telephones may have been around for many years, but not everyone was linked to the utilities, especially older folk who may not have the money or inclination to pay from home improvements. Before mains water became the norm water was as a matter of course taken from the local well or village pump. The village pump at May Bank is clearly still providing a sterling service for one of the area's senior residents. Even a single mains water cold tap remained a luxury for some folk for many more years, never mind a bathroom and a flushing toilet. Even by the 1970s some houses still had outside toilets and no bathrooms despite a century of work by local authorities.

Right: This 1918 photograph shows the newly built Cobden Street, in Dresden when the town of Longton was still prospering and expanding its suburbs. Beyond the trees at the top of the street and out of view is Florence Colliery, an industrial scene that this image belies. Notice the small frontages and bay windows on the left closest to the photographer. These would have classified this part of the street as 'white collar', whilst the other houses without bay windows would have been for those further down the social scale. Note also the small off-licence and chapel, both very important features in an Edwardian middle class area.

question that at one time, Longton was the Potteries' capital of public houses. This very early picture shows inquisitive onlookers on Stafford Street outside The Glass Barrel (later renamed The Rose and Crown). The view is looking along Stafford Street towards Longton and a little further along was The Robin Hood pub and half way down the street are two men and a cart at the junction with Commerce Street. The building on the bottom corner of the junction is the John Tams Crown Works pottery.

Above: Longton ('long village') is a market town in the parish of Stoke and is the newest of the six towns to evolve. In March 1865, Longton and Lane End were incorporated as the Borough of Longton. Rapid industrial growth and a polluted environment inevitably led at the time, to ill health, poverty and poor housing. The local public houses were one place you could go to while away the hours over a glass of ale. There is no

Below: Stafford Street which runs from The Strand in Longton town centre at one end to a roundabout on the A50 Trunk road at the other end. Before the building of the A50 Stafford Street joined Lightwood Road. In the early 1950s this lower part of Stafford Street was renamed "The Strand". In this picture, to the right can be seen the French Renaissance style, grand entrance towers of Longton indoor market. At the bottom of the road the landmark railway bridge can been seen.

This part of Newcastle was originally a marsh that was drained during the 18th century to create new land on which to build. Nelson Place was created to provide a central point at which six roads met. The photograph shows what Nelson Place and the bottom end of the Ironmarket looked like in 1937. The small ornate roundabout was the forerunner of the substantial fountains roundabout. Queen Victoria's statue is seen in its original position, before it was moved to Station Walks and then to the Queen's Gardens in 2001. The statue was given to the town in 1903 by Sir Alfred Haslem and was unveiled by the Grand Duke Michael of Russia, to celebrate the coronation of Edward VII.

Above: Stoke-on-Trent Railway Station is located opposite the North Stafford Hotel in Winton Square. This very fine Grade II listed Victorian station was built by the North Staffordshire Railway Company for just over £30,000 and was opened on 9 October, 1848. Built in brick and sandstone to a beautifully detailed Elizabethan and Jacobean design.

Stoke-on-Trent has always been and still is the hub of North Staffordshire's passenger train service. The station provides an interchange between various local services running through Cheshire, Staffordshire and Derbyshire. The station building retains much of its mid-Victorian character, including a classic glazed roof that spans the platforms.

Left and right: The picture right, from 1928, could have been taken from outside a car showroom, but it is actually in front of the North Stafford Hotel, Winton Square, Stoke. The Victorian station buildings were opened on 9 October, 1848. The other buildings located in Winton Square, including the North Stafford Hotel (originally The Railway Hotel) a Grade II listed building, were opened in June, 1849. All were constructed by John Jay to the design of H.A. Hunt, of London, using an architectural style referred to as

'robust Jacobean manor-house'. The station was built by the North Staffordshire Railway Company and, until the amalgamation of 1923, housed the Company's Boardroom and its principal offices. Stoke-on-Trent has always been and still is the hub of North Staffordshire's passenger train service. The statue to the left is of Josiah Wedgwood, born in Burslem in 1730. He is depicted wearing contemporary dress of frock coat, buckled shoes, breeches and wig. He holds a copy of the Portland Vase, a Roman artefact in glass. The apparent reason for siting the work in front of the railway station, rather than anywhere more central, was that it would therefore be on the boundary of Hanley and Stoke-on-Trent, both of whom laid claim to being the home of Wedgwood. The statue was unveiled by the Earl of Harrow at a ceremony which included processions from each of Stoke-on-Trent's six towns, and an extravagant meal for the gathered dignitaries at the North Stafford Hotel.

Below: Spot the difference. Two photos of the Black Lion public house in Broad Street, Hanley, taken some decades apart. The Black Lion Inn is at the junction of Robson Street, just by the roundabout on Hanley ring road 'The Potteries Way'. In 1949, when the first photograph was taken, Broad Street is almost empty of traffic. How many vehicles can you count? Just three travelling along the road, three or four more parked and a bus in the far distance. Those were the days when motorists took it for granted that they could park outside whatever shop they wished to visit. Alas, they are long gone: the double yellow lines outside the pub in the second picture tell a tale all of their own. As for the pub itself, superficially not much has changed. The signs have been replaced but it's still the same building. Yet other changes have been more subtle: the old frosted glass has been replaced by net curtains. In 1949 all pubs featured frosted glass windows – it wouldn't do to let children and wives see what was going on inside. Certainly there was many a pint of Burton's drunk in what was then the 'public bar' at the Black Lion. Marston's Burton Bitter is one of the company's oldest beers, amongst the first created by

John Marston when he established his brewery in Burton-on-Trent in 1834. In 1949, however, the price of a pint was barely five pence in modern money. A far cry from today's prices.

Above: This photo taken in the 1930s shows the small terraced housing that was typical of the kind of living accommodation shared by thousands in Newcastle in the first half of the 20th Century.In the second half of the century these homes, and many more like them, were demolished and the inhabitants were offered new council houses to live in. Not everyone was pleased to be moved however. The old houses may have been damp, with no gardens and no bathrooms, some may have been infested with vermin. But on the other hand they were handy for work, often built within a few yards of the factory entrance. There was seldom any need for long commuting journeys in those days. And everyone knew everyone else. Neighbours were never strangers in those far off times. People looked after one another in a way seldom experienced today. And it was safe to play in the street as the youngsters pictured here demonstrate so well. By the time they were responsible adults in the 1960s vast swathes of old properties like those in Ball's Yard were bulldozed to make way for new roads and housing developments. Ball's Yard now exists only in the memories of some of our oldest residents.

Above: A view of Howard Place taken in 1950 makes Shelton look like an idyllic country village of the kind which featured so frequently in old British black and white films of the period made by Ealing Studios. Not a motor car in sight, just an iconic rear-entrance double decker bus, and in the distance a horse and cart – inevitably passing in front of a half-timbered building. A Hollywood producer would have probably over-egged the pudding and asked for a church in the background to establish the shot, and a couple of Belisha beacons thrown in good measure, not to mention two or three good-looking children to give the scene some life.

Bottom left: If the clock above Burslem's old town hall is to be believed it's twenty-five past eleven on this sunny morning outside the Midland Bank. By 1950 when this photo was taken Belisha beacons had long been a familiar sight. They took their odd-sounding name from Leslie Hore-Belisha (1895-1957), the Minister of Transport who in 1934 added beacons to pedestrian crossings, which were then marked by large metal studs in the road surface. These crossings were later painted in black and white stripes, inevitably becoming known as zebra cossings. The former town hall topped by its famous angel was eventually relegated for use as a public library. It was built in 1854-7 on the site of the town's first town hall. The massive stone building was designed by G. T. Robinson, of Wolverhampton, in a mixture of classical styles. At the west end is a projecting portico with arched entrances below and free-standing Corinthian columns. Above this the clock tower is supported by caryatid figures, the whole being crowned by the gilded angel, a noted Burslem landmark. Internally there is an impressive entrance hall at the west end featuring tall cast-iron columns and a double staircase.

Below: Readers will have many fond memories of shopping at Lewis's - the building on the left with the clock. Do you remember the food hall window on Stafford Street that was piled high with ring doughnuts every Saturday? And taking the children along to see Santa Claus in his grotto at Christmas? The cash room known as the 'tube room' was a feature peculiar to Lewis's; money from departments without a till was sent to the tube room where the assistant on duty, meticulously dressed in black and white, took the cash and gave out the change. Lewis's acquired the building that fronted Stafford Street and Miles Bank in 1935 at a cost of £250,000, and the department store remained a favourite with shoppers for many years. On the corner, in front of Lewis's is the Fifty Shilling Tailors, a British chain of shops selling men's clothes. Founded in Leeds in 1905 by Henry Price, the chain expanded to over 399 stores across the country. In 1958 the company was sold to UDS, which renamed it John Collier. It continued to trade within the UDS empire until 1983 when UDS was acquired by Hanson plc. In 1985 the company was purchased by the Burton Group, but the brand was discontinued and no longer exists today. Many of the buildings in this photograph were cleared for the new Potteries Shopping Centre, opened in the late 1980s. The streets to the right are pedestrian shopping precincts today, while Stafford Street is part of the city's one-way system.

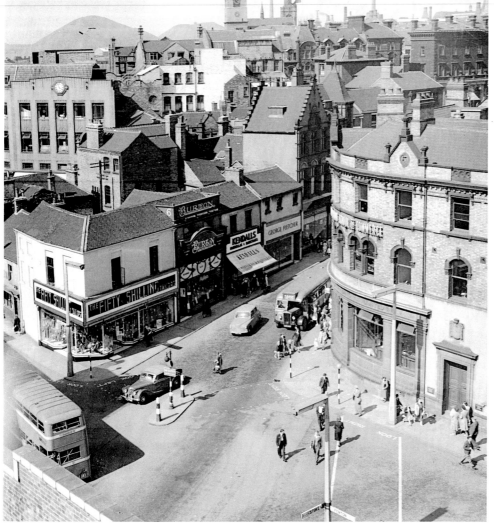

Below: Whilst the buildings on the left and right of this scene remain, all those in the centre have been demolished. This picture was taken one sunny lunchtime in 1956. The cameraman is in an elevated position in the Queen's Hall in Wedgwood Street, looking south down Market Place, in Burslem. To the far left is the former Town Hall which was superseded in civic importance by the Queen's Hall. There are six listed buildings in Market Place including four shops, the Leopard Inn, and of course, the old town hall. The mid-1950s were a time of optimism for Burslem folk. As Prime Minister Harold Macmillan would famously remark a couple of years later, many people 'had never had it so good'.

Right: It's 1966, the height of the 'Swinging Sixties', and if popular music is to be believed then 'revolution is in the air'. This photographer was certainly up in the air. It's a photo of Nelson Place was taken from the top of the Municipal Hall before it was demolished. And if you're looking for a revolution, how about a circuit of the traffic roundabout? Many things have changed recently: On the land between Kings Street

and Brunswick Street the Plaza Cinema has been demolished to make way for an office block. At a later date the bottom floor of this building was bricked up to provide extra accommodation. To the right, just out of view, are the swimming baths built in 1906. Newly absent from this view is the statue of Queen Victoria which once occupied the centre of Nelson Place. To make way for road widening in Nelson Place in 1963 the statue was moved to Station Walks in 1963, where it remained until 2001. The Newcastle Civic Society pressed for the statue to be restored and moved to the Queen's Gardens. Members successfully bid for a £10,000 millennium grant to achieve this, and the statue was unveiled in its new location in July 2001 - returned close to its original home in Nelson Place.

Above: On Piccadilly can be seen the Abbey National Building Society, while just in front cars can be seen on the roof of John Peppers garage which fronted Piccadilly, with workshops extending into Albion Street. Just to the right of centre (behind John Peppers) the top of the Regent Theatre can be seen. On the sky line (middle left) the tower of St. John's Church on High Street (now Town Road) is visible. On the corner of Piccadilly and Marsh Street (extreme left) stands the shop of Harris 'Electrical Engineers'; the shop is called 'Electricity House'. The ornate building on the far right is the 'Staffs and Potteries Water Board Offices'. At the junction of Albion and Bethesda Street - this is a listed building. The car park is that belonging to the Potteries Museum. On this site stood the Bell Pottery, but the area was cleared in the mid 1950s.

Right: This is an aerial view of Trentham Gardens, a formal Italianate gardens and an English landscape park in Trentham, on the southern fringes of Stoke-on-Trent. A serpentine park, designed by Lancelot Brown (more commonly known as Capability Brown) in 1759, with a nineteenth century terrace garden. The house was demolished in 1911 by its owner the 4th Duke of Sutherland and Trentham Gardens is now a public park. Sir Charles Barry designed an Italian garden beside the lake in 1840. His design has been simplified, but survives. The gardens and park at Trentham currently cover some 300 acres and in 2004 were restored and re-opened under the name Trentham Leisure.

Above: Tunstall is the most northern town of the city. Historians have found that iron was being produced there as far back as 1280. It stands on a ridge surrounded by old tilemaking and brickmaking sites, some of which probably date back to the late Middle Ages. This view along Furlong Road looks from Christ Church at the top of Tunstall High Street towards Pittshill. The bridge in the picture carries a spur line used to transport raw materials (clay, etc) to Newfield Pottery via Tunstall. The Loop Line bridge is out of sight over the next hill.

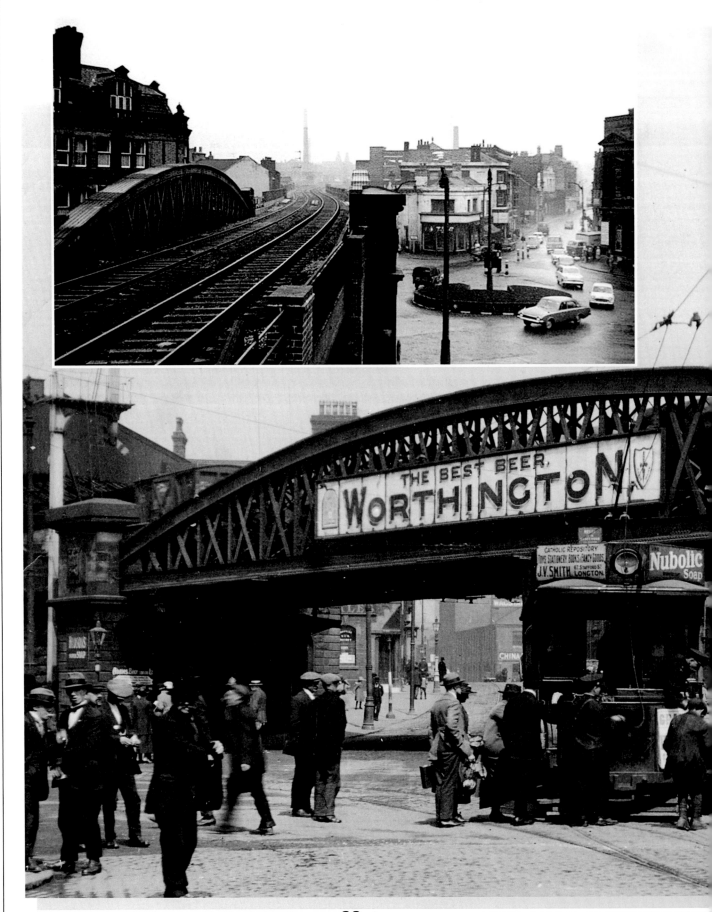

The image top left is of Times Square, in Longton, around 1968. To the left is the Crown & Anchor Hotel and off to the right is Market Street. The junction of what became Market Place (and now called Times Square) had, by the 17th century taken on a name of its own: Meir Lane End, later abbreviated to Lane End. For many years this was regarded as a separate township to Longton. However, the name Lane End was to fade away during the 19th century as the two communities became one. The origins of the Crown & Anchor (The Crown), located on King Street, go back to the early 1800s with the present building being built in 1887. Situated opposite the Town Hall, the hotel continues to provide friendly service with no frills, comfortable accommodation and is universally known among The Potteries. Rooms located on the first or second floor of this Victorian building retain many of the original features. The bridge (completed in 1889) carries the Crewe to Derby railway. Behind the bridge on the right is the Crown & Anchor and just behind the hotel can be seen the tower of St. John's Church. Longton railway station is served by East Midlands trains on the Crewe to Derby line. The station was opened on 7 August, 1848, by the North Staffordshire Railway. It is located on an embankment opposite the town hall and next to the cantilever bridge, which is a local landmark.

EVENTS & OCCASIONS

This dramatic photograph captures the scene on 21st April, 1929, during the erection of a railway bridge in the north of Stoke-on Trent. A crowd has gathered to watch events unfold on this fine Sunday morning. The only surprise is that the crowd is so small: in the days before television almost any out of the ordinary event could attract hundreds of spectators. Wisely the crowd is being kept well back for

in the days before Health and safety legislation accidents of all kinds were common. The steam locomotive on the embankment is one of hundreds of sturdy little engines used in such unglamorous roles and working constantly in the shunting yards. Not for them the glory of steam age. Eclipsed by the excitement on the railway embankment is the telegraph pole in the centre of the scene. The extraordinary number of wires which the pole is designed to carry provides ample evidence of the ever increasing demand for telephone communication over the preceding forty years. Today such extensively festooned poles are rare as more and more lines are placed underground. In the 1920s, and for decades afterwards, however telephone lines would clutter the landscape to a degree now unimaginable.

Mayor and Mayoress Knowles welcoming Scottish Olympic swimmer Cathie Gibson to the King Edward VII baths in Newcastle (below). Catherine Brown, née Gibson, born 21 March, 1931, was using the swimming baths for training. Also pictured is Harry Roskie and some of the swimming bath staff. The swimming baths were built in 1906 to commemorate the coronation of King Edward VII. They have been improved on a number of occasions and were renamed the Jubilee swimming baths in 2002. Gibson represented Great Britain at the 1948 Summer Olympic Games, held in London. She competed in the 100m backstroke, 400m individual medley, 4x100m freestyle relay and the 400m freestyle, in which she won the bronze medal in a time of 5 minutes 22.5 s. She also competed at the European Championships in 1947, collecting two silver medals. In 2008 she was inducted into the Scottish Sports Hall of Fame.

Below: An excited group of royal watchers and yet there's no monarch in sight. This photograph was taken in High Street, Chesterton on 2 June, 1953. Many of the youngsters at the front will have vivid recollections of the occasion. For the first time

ever, the ordinary people of Britain were able to watch a Monarch's Coronation. It was announced earlier in the year that the crowning of the Queen would be televised. As a result sales of television sets soared. In fact there had been considerable controversy as to whether it would be appropriate to televise such a solemn occasion. Several members of the Cabinet, Sir Winston Churchill amongst them, urged the Queen to spare herself the strain of the heat and glare of the cameras. Happily Her Majesty and refused to listen. All over the country at 11 o'clock people settled down in front of their, or more likely their neighbour's, television sets. These sets were primitive compared to the present day digital TVs. The grainy 405-line pictures were black and white, and a tiny 14-inch screen was 'state of the art'. Street parties were held all over the country to mark the new Elizabethan era.

Right: Local youngsters are playing their part in the Wedgwood Pageant. In 1930, to celebrate the 200th anniversary of the birth of Josiah Wedgwood, Hanley Park became the centre for the celebrations. There was plenty to recall and give thanks for. Wedgwood and his fellow potters had provided work for the residents and development for the region since the middle of the 18th century. People turned out in their thousands to mark their appreciation of the Potteries' unique way of life. But it was not an event limited to local residents. People booked train tickets and boarded 'charas' from far and wide to join in the fun. The travel agent, Thomas Cook, advertised the event nationally and the floodgates opened. The pageant ran for a full week in May. Every new day saw a different chapter in history being acted out. The carnival kicked off with the Druids and, all through the week, a cast of 5,000 acted out historical scenes. In celebration of local industry there just had to be a pottery tableau included. About 1,500 local workers made it a tableau to be remembered. The entertainment went on late into the evenings with a military tattoo, dancing, fireworks, concerts and a torchlight display. The children's gymnastics display that you are looking at had 3,000 youngsters participating.

Hanley's annual Pageant of Queens was always something to look forward to. Most towns make do with just one carnival Queen, but there were too many beautiful girls in Hanley in the 1950s to make choosing a single one an option here in Hanley Park. In the end, however, just one of the queens was crowned the Pottery Queen. Hanley Park was the venue for the week-long Wedgwood bicentenary pageant of 1930, which was attended by 70,000 people and was undoubtedly one of the great outdoor events in local history. The event included the crowning of the Pottery Queen following a

contest entered each year by hundreds of girls working on potbanks. One of the local beauties at the festival of queens in 1937 was Elsie Ashley, later mayor of Newcastle and a public figure of longstanding. As Elsie Lucas, a miner's daughter from Silverdale, she was the village's carnival queen. The Pottery Queen was the modern industrial equivalent of ancient rural traditions which are deeply embedded in the human psyche. Meanwhile it was a proud day for the girls here chosen as Queen for the day. Something to boast about for the rest of their lives.

Right and below: These pictures were taken less than 2 miles from each other, on the same day in 1953. The common theme to the photographs was a celebration to mark the accession to the throne of Queen Elizabeth II. The Queen replaced her father, King George VI, as monarch following his death on 6 February 1952. After 16 years on the throne he passed away in his sleep and his 25-year-old daughter Elizabeth immediately became Queen. The princess formally proclaimed herself Queen and Head of the Commonwealth and Defender of the Faith in February 1952 but the amount of planning and a wish for a sunny day for the occasion led to the long but excited wait for this day. The celebration day eventually arrived on 2 June 1953, with many thousands of processions and street parties taking place up and down

ahead at the camera. He has still not quite managed it, but it was a worthy effort. With party hats in place the group was formed in the rear playground at the lower end of the school. The school was originally opened in 1854 by Earl Granville and has now been replaced by Forest Park Primary School.

Below: By the 1960s, traffic congestion was a major problem in Stoke-on-Trent, and journeys across the area sometimes took hours. There was no connection from the newly constructed M6 to the city. Businesses in the area wanted an easier route to get their goods out of the area. The A500 was built from the M6 at junction 16 to the A34 road at Talke as part of the

the country. The first picture shows the procession making its way down Vincent Street in Northwood. Vincent Street ran from Cardwell Street to Botany Bay Road, but this part of the street no longer exists. The houses were very poor quality and badly maintained, each had it's own outside lavatory at the bottom of a small patch of enclosed yard or garden at the back of the house. The small children at the front are carrying a plate and spoon for the feast of jelly hopefully waiting at the end of the procession.

I am not sure how long it would have taken the photographer of the second picture to organize this smartly dressed group of schoolchildren from Granville Street School. It could have been quite a lengthy process to get them all to stand still and look straight

motorway construction, opening in 1962. At the southern end, a dual carriageway was constructed from junction 15 of the M6 to the A34 near Trentham, given the number A5006, and opened at the same time. The northern section of the road was then subsequently extended from Talke to the A53 road. Work started in 1974 to the final section and this picture shows the official opening of the Etruria to Hanford section in 1977. Construction involved the destruction of streets and businesses within Stoke's town centre, as well as the excavation of a mass grave of the victims of a 17th-century cholera epidemic. This final section was named Queensway, and on its completion the whole route became the A500. Because of its shape between the motorway junctions, it is known locally as the D-Road (D is also the Roman numeral representing the number 500).

Below: The Newcastle carnival was an annual Bank Holiday Monday attraction for 30 years, after the octocentenary carnival celebrations of 1973. This modern-day equivalent of the pageants of Tudor times was watched by crowds of up to 30,000. An enjoyable community event with a carnival atmosphere was the order of the day. Many people would wear fancy dress costumes, including dignitaries like the mayor and mayoress The event went on all day and included a procession by dozens of floats, charity stalls, a fun fair and many live entertainers and music performances. Unfortunately for the good folk of Newcastle-under-Lyme and surrounding areas, the good times were to come to an end. Health and safety issues along with the cost of public liability insurance cover, brought about the demise of the event.

TRANSPORT

Above: This photograph shows an electric tram and its operatives around 1920. The conductor and the driver of the tram are wearing thick, heavy coats to guard themselves from bad weather. There is a poster on the front of the tram advertising the Theatre Royal's production of The Scarlet Pimpernel. Electric trams were used until around the mid 1920s.

Left: The inauguration of the first tram service to reach Newcastle. The service was run by the Potteries Electric Traction Company. All of the company's tram's were single-deckers, like the ones in the photograph, because of the many low bridges in the area. Services ran from Newcastle to Burslem, Chesterton, Hanley, Silverdale, and Wolstanton. Trams were a popular form of transport until 1928 when they were superseded by the bus service. The Municipal Hall can be seen near the bottom of the Ironmarket on the left hand side. Bayley and Son can just be seen on the left hand side of the street, which was a confectioners, and tea rooms.

Above: The motor car was the very thing in 1925 when this sunny scene was captured for posterity. Behind the parked cars is Beeston's Vaults, in Red Lion Square, Newcastle, premises more recently known as the Wine Vaults. The original building dates from the 17th century and has a timber-framed structure. Beeston's Vaults took its name from the Beeston family. The pub had been run by that family since the 1860s and it remained a Beeston family business until late in the century. For those who deemed alcohol sinful (in the 1920s the teetotal movement was still a force to be reckoned with) and for those ladies for whom going into a pub for drink was a shocking idea, the café next door offered a welcome alternative. The picture is of particular note since it manages to combine three competing modes of transport, not only the trio of cars but also a horse on the left and, in the foreground a tram track. Few in 1925 would have felt certain about predicting which means of transport would prove the most enduring. Motor cars may have been becoming increasingly popular, but in the 1920s, despite the best efforts of the likes of Messrs Morris and Ford, owning a car was still far beyond the means of working folk, for whom even a bicycle on which to ride to work was a luxury many could not afford. Who back then could have predicted the enormous number of cars on our roads today?

Below: In the 1920s steam was still king. Our picture captures the scene in the locomotive yard at Stoke Roundhouse in Stoke-on-Trent. The men standing proudly in front of the engine are locomotive engineers and the NSR company managers. The North Staffordshire Railway was widely known as the 'Knotty' after the Staffordshire Knot crest initially used by the company as an heraldic device. The Knotty came into being in 1845 as a result of the amalgamation of the Staffordshire Potteries and Churnet Valley Railways. The first section of the railway opened for goods traffic in April 1848. Passenger services commenced two weeks later. The first section extended from Stoke-on-Trent to Norton Bridge (a few miles north of Stafford on the LNWR's route). NSR lines extended from Macclesfield to Norton Bridge, and from Crewe Junction to North Stafford Junction, located between Burton-on-Trent and Derby. A branch from this line led to Burton-on-Trent. A second major route was from North Rode, just south of Macclesfield, via the Churnet Valley to Uttoxeter. A job on the railways was believed to a passport to work for life. Small boys aspired to be engine drivers when they grew up – no doubt inspired by the fact that a railway engine was the fastest thing they had ever seen. Diesel and electric locomotives were still undreamed of when these men posed for the camera.

Left: Church Street, Audley, in the 1920s. Johnson's buses are lined up outside Carryer's pawnbrokers shop. The buses are already full of folk ready for the off. At the front is a bus conductor loaded up with his money bag and ticket machine. The more economically efficient one-man operated bus made its first appearance in the late 1960s and today is almost universal. Until then however every bus had both a driver to drive and a conductor to collect fares. 'Move on down the bus please' and 'I thank you' became catch phrases. 'Sorry I haven't anything smaller' as one offered a half-crown (two shillings and sixpence, or 12 1/2p) for a fivepenny fare always drew a malevolent smile from the conductor: it was the opportunity to get rid of some weight by giving the unlucky passenger change in what seemed like a ton of copper coinage - farthings, ha'pennies, and pennies – and in those pre-decimal days a penny was the size of a cart wheel!

Above: Swan Bank, Burslem. It's the early 1920s and the modern age has arrived. Just a generation previously this scene would have looked very different. Thirty years earlier there would have been no cars, no tram and no war memorial. For the people of not only Burslem, but of the whole of Britain, technology and war had changed everything. The adults in this picture grew up in a very different Burslem, one in which the horse was still king of the road, and only railways offered the chance to travel at speed. Every adult in Burslem would be able to recall the first time they saw a motor car, and the first time they saw an electric light. Trams were the harbingers of electrical power to some localities. Since trams ran off electricity it was often the tram companies which installed the first power cables in urban areas, which in turn allowed the public to 'electrify' their homes for the first time. Goodbye gas mantle, hello electric light bulb! Sadly the technology which made life better also made it worse. Industrial mass production not only made cars and trams but also machine guns, artillery and bombs.

Left: This picture from 1947 shows the two double deckers passing along Moorland Road to the junction at Swan Square. Moorland Road runs from Smallthorne Roundabout at the junction of Hanley Road and High Lane, at the top; down to Burslem town centre at the bottom. The building on the right is now a branch of Lloyds Bank and to the left is The Red Lion, which is where Robbie Williams spent his formative childhood years.

Right: It's High Street in Newcastle and the traffic is nose to tail. Like so many towns nothing had prepared the civic authorities for the incredible increase in traffic volume which would arise in the boom years of the 1950s. Most English towns had been built astride main roads, at cross roads and river crossings. No one had ever planned them as such, they had just grown naturally. Roads had actually become less important as the centuries had passed. The construction of canals in the 18th century had taken much heavy traffic off the existing highways. In the 19th century the most modern of rapid transport systems, the railways, had threatened to make roads and road travel obsolete for all but the shortest journeys. Even in the early years of the 20th century roads simply provided convenient routes upon which tram tracks could be laid. How wrong those folk turned out to be who ever thought that roads were the past rather than the future! Despite an economic downturn in the 1920s, and world-wide depression in the 1930s, motor car production never faltered. Only the Second World War

with petrol rationing and factories turned over to war work offered a brief respite. This picture taken in the late 1950s reveals a terrible tale of traffic congestion which was eased in the following decade only by the construction of the ring road.

Below: Author Kenneth Grahame (1859-1932) is best remembered for his 1908 book 'Wind in the Willows'. The driver of this 1933 car might just have been modelled on Mr Toad. It is certainly the type of tourer that would have got the old boy's heart racing, as well as the engine. He would happily speed along the lanes, shouting 'What fun!' and fun it must have been in real life for the owner of such a car. Britain's roads were not cluttered with traffic as they became later on and it was easy to find an open stretch of road and just let rip. This fine example of craftsmanship, was registered in 1933. Younger readers might look at the front of the car and observe a small hole at the bottom of the radiator grille and wonder as to its use. This was where a starting handle was inserted and the engine cranked over if the so-called self-starting button or interior switch did not succeed in stirring the car into life.

A Potteries Motor Traction bus bound for Silverdale is bought to a halt by a police constable in Hartshill. Public transport was still popular around this time and although becoming more widely used, cars were still luxury items and not everybody felt the need to own their own vehicle. Police officers on point duty were a common sight before the advent of electronic traffic controls. At the time women police officers were desperate for equality but this was to prove difficult given the constrictions of the women's uniforms. Female officers' uniforms have gone through a great variety of styles, as they have tended to reflect the women's fashions of the time. A soft hat, handbag, A-line skirt and nylon stockings, was not necessarily the best attire for chasing criminals through the back streets of Stoke. They did look very smart however, and this policewoman could be one of the first to wear the new styled uniform designed by Norman Hartnell, dressmaker to the Royal family.

POTTERIES LIFE

Anyone born in the Potteries at the start of the 20th century would have lived to see more changes in their lifetime than any generation before or since. The first year of the new century saw the end of an era, the Victorian Age, marked by the death of Queen Victoria. Few then living could recall a time when she had not been on the throne. In the new century technology would see cars replace horses, men take to the air in flying machines, and the arrival of the BBC and 'wireless' radio broadcasting. Two world wars saw both tragedy and triumph, the abuse of industrial technology to destroy the lives of millions, but also the advancement of science to a previously undreamt of degree. Yet in the first half of the twentieth century only a few would see real benefits from advances in science and technology. For most working folk the decades were more likely to be marked by varying degrees of poverty rather than affluence. Real improvements in most people's standard of living had to wait until the second half of the century. In the Potteries folk were often just glad to have a decent job and enough money to pay the rent or the doctor's bill. None born in 1901 would have ever thought that their children or grandchildren might one day fly in jet planes to the Mediterranean for their Wakes holidays.

Above: Seen here are the Hall family outside Halls Model Lodging house in Union Street, Hanley. The man in the cart is Samuel Knapper Hall II, with his grandson Albert and the two women in the doorway are Sam's daughter, Violet and his daughter-in-law, Ellen Hall, nee Toft. The Model Lodging House provided for itinerant workers who could not afford expensive accommodation. In the 1891 census the Halls were in residence, along with 79 lodgers, whose ages varied between 9 and 71, and it was officially called Halls Model Lodging House. It was demolished in the 60s to make way for the Potteries Way.

Right: From the 18th century until the 1960s, bottle ovens were the dominating feature of the Staffordshire Potteries. There were over two thousand of them standing at any one time and they could be seen everywhere one looked. Some small factories had only one bottle oven, other large potbanks had as many as twenty-five. Within a factory ovens were not situated according to any set plan. They might be grouped around a cobbled yard or placed in a row. Sometimes they were built into the workshops with the upper part of the chimney protruding through the roof. No two bottle ovens were exactly alike. They were all built according to the whim of the builder or of the potbank owner. The kilns in the foreground look like calcining type. There is no particular reason a calcining kiln should be bottle shaped, since it is used not to fire pottery, but to prepare the flint and animal bones which are added to clay to make up the material from which pottery is made. This material is called the body. Before the flint or animal bones can be added to the body, they have to be crushed to a fine powder. If they are burnt or calcined, they become brittle and can be powdered with ease.

Above: This is a view of Mersey Weaver Wharf, alongside the Burslem branch canal. The skyline is dominated by dozens of smoky bottle kilns and is the district known as Dale Hall, between Burslem and Longport. When the canal was authorised by an Act of Parliament in 1797, it paved the way for Burslem to become the cornerstone for ceramic production. Construction work was completed in 1805, 30 years after James Brindley completed the adjoining Trent and Mersey Canal. Large quantities of china clay, stone and other raw materials were shipped in for use at the Burslem potbanks and finished ware was exported via the River Mersey and Liverpool Docks. The canal was even immortalised by Arnold Bennett when Denry Machin's horse and cart crashed into it in his novel 'The Card'. The canal had been built lock-free on the summit pound of the

Trent and Mersey but was on the side of a deep, narrow valley. The embankment failed in December 1961 and the ensuing breach was devastating and as a result the branch canal was formally closed and infilled.

Bottom left: The Mersey Weaver Wharf in the 1930s. East View is the row of terrace houses on the left hand side of the canal. In the distance is the tower of St. Paul's Church.

Below: The world may be at war, but here at the Wedgwood factory in 1941 it is still business as usual thanks to the company's dedicated team of ladies who are busy decorating pottery. Part of a 382 acre estate, the Wedgwood factory was built near the village of Barlaston, south of Stoke-on-Trent. The land was purchased by the Wedgwood family in 1936 for the site of the building. The architects for the new factory were Keith Murray and his partner Charles White. The foundation stone was laid on 10 September, 1938. Earthenware production was transferred from the old Etruria site in 1940, with production officially ending at Etruria on 13 June, 1950. At the time it was completed the new Barlaston factory was the most advanced pottery in Britain, and firing was powered by electricity in the Brown Boveri tunnel ovens.

Above: Young paintresses in the Enamel Department at Beswick's Gold Street Works, in Longton, decorate the popular 'Palm Tree' series, Christmas 1950.

Broad Street runs from the bottom of Piccadilly in the centre of Hanley and joins Snow Hill near St. Marks Church in Shelton. Halfway down its length Broad Street now has a roundabout which joins it to Hanley's ring road "The Potteries Way".

This house looks like it could have come straight from the set of the Addams Family. It is however the workplace of Whitmore Dentistry, Broad Street, in the late 1890s. This was a well known, quality establishment. A trades review at the time suggested, "They have the finest show of teeth in the Potteries" (over 6,000 natural teeth and many thousands of artificial ones) and that because of modern

Painless Extractions!

ARTIFICIAL TEETH!

WEEKLY PAYMENTS TAKEN.

WHITMORE & CO.,
78, BROAD STREET,
HANLEY,

(Late Whitmore & Son. Dental Surgeons).
Also partners of the late C. Hoyland.
Dental Surgeon.

In attendance, H. WHITMORE,
and W. MORRIS, Surgeon Dentist.

appliances and remedies, "they have robbed a visit to this establishment of half its terrors". By definition, this still means the other half could have been an absolute nightmare, which we can only imagine. Remember, during the Middle Ages and throughout the 19th century, dentistry was not a profession in itself, and often dental procedures were performed by barbers or general physicians who used the most basic extraction instruments. Mr Cyrus Whitmore, who died around the time of this photograph, was obviously an early pioneer of the profession.

Below: This stunning aerial view of Hanley was taken in the late 1950s. Looking north across the town, there are many landmarks that the famous son of Hanley, Sir Stanley Matthews, would have recognised. Soccer's first footballing knight was born in Seymour Street on 1 February, 1915, not far from the Caldon Canal, to the east of the photograph. He would have recalled many of the sights that have now changed forever. Broad Street comes into view at the bottom as it turns past Swinnertons. The factory grew around the bottle ovens, so that only their chimneys looked out above the rooftop. College Road runs off to the right towards Stoke station. The entrance to Shelton Church, St Mark's, is opposite the Victoria Pottery. Evans Halshaw's garage later commanded most of the old factory area. Much of the scene is now greatly changed. At the top left, beyond where the prefabs stood, the Potteries Shopping Centre is now dominant. The grand old man died in 2000. Swinnertons Victoria Pottery is on the corner of Broad Street and Victoria Road (now College Road). The Victoria pottery works was originally built in 1864 and run by John Adams & Co., later owned by Elijah Cotton and subsequently Swinnertons. In 1925, the Victoria Pottery was purchased by Swinnertons, followed soon after by the purchase of the Scotia Pottery at Burslem.

Below: This 1930 photograph shows Lower John Street, off the main John Street, in Longton. One can clearly see the squalid conditions in which many people in England's industrial towns had to live. However, notice the clean white washing amongst the backdrop of smokey bottle ovens. Also note the makeshift wall made of old saggars, a vessel used to contain and protect pottery during firing. It can be seen behind the second row of washing.

Right, facing page: The Bell Pottery, Bethesda Street, Hanley, in 1953, this viewed looking along Bethesda Street. The kilns of the Bell Pottery are being demolished to make way for a new Museum and Art Gallery which opened in 1956. To the left is a group of buildings which were part of the former Staffordshire Potteries Water Board, and further left is the Sunday School of the Bethesda Methodist Chapel. The Blue Bell stood on the corner of Broad Street and Warner Street in Hanley. The hostelry was notable as the first pub to be run by Stoke City and England footballer Neil Franklin, who took the licence in around 1952. Franklin was to be the last landlord of the Blue Bell, as the pub was demolished shortly after this photograph was taken to make way for the first stage of what is now the Potteries Museum and Art Gallery.

Below: The building of the Caldon Canal through Milton in 1777 was important to the village's later development. In particular, packing houses for finished pottery ware were established at Milton adjacent to the canal. One of the major companies to transport finished ware from their factory in Hanley to Milton was Johnson Brothers. At the time, Johnson's used three narrowboats all incorporating Milton in their name: The Milton Queen, The Milton Maid and The Milton Princess. In the 1970s, Johnson Brothers realised that the carriage of delicate china ware between their different factory sites would be less damaging if carried out by water on the adjacent Caldon Canal. Using two purpose-built catamaran-style vessels, crates of china were carried around a quarter of a mile. So successful was the project that catamarans Milton Maid and Milton Queen were supplemented by the more conventional-style narrowboat Milton Princess, seen here on its inaugural run in 1979. The operation continued until 1995 when Milton Maid carried the last load from Johnson's Imperial Works to the Eagle Works. Imperial Works closed shortly afterwards and was demolished.

Above: What's this cheeky boy want? Who could refuse him anything? A grand little chap, no doubt well into his autumn years now, but pictured here with his mother and 'Mrs-Next-Door'. This scene would have been repeated a thousand times a day in the early 1950s. Two neighbours chatting over the fence. Children playing on the cobbles and net curtains at the windows. Washing is hung out to dry, whilst chimney pots almost next to the washing are poised at any moment to begin spewing out smoke and soot turning the whole exercise futile. 'Pinnies', short for pinafores, were almost mandatory for housewives, though the lady on the right appears to have forgotten to put hers on. She has however made up for the omission by wrapping a scarf round her hair – another common sight, and one which often hid, or more often failed to hide, hair-curlers. These were days when having a 'perm' – short for 'permanent wave' - was still the fashion. Those with the money could go to a hairdresser to have the deed done. Those with less cash settled for a DIY 'home-perm'. Attached to the house wall at the corner is a gas lamp. Not phased out until the 1960s, the corner streetlight cast a warm circle of light under which children gathered to play in the darker evenings. Later on in the evening those a little older would gather under it to do their courting, until fathers and mothers called their daughters into the house.

Below: What a lovely smile! One of the oft-encountered frustrations in scouring the archives is the discovery of a picture with almost no details. This photograph is just one such intriguing picture. Who was this girl? Where was it taken? And what happened to her in later life? We know that the scene is a local one. Written on the back is 'Pottery Worker's Daughter – 1950s'. How tantalising. The girl must be around 12 years old. She was probably born just after the war – the first of the 'baby-boomers', that great cohort of children who were all born in 1946, 1947 and 1948. During six years of war millions of husbands and wives had been separated by service in the forces and by distance. Now, in a time a peace, lost ground was being made up. This anonymous face represents all those who would grow up knowing nothing of the two wars their parents and grandparents had endured. Hers was a future not just of peace but of affluence and relative plenty. Around the time this photo was taken Prime Minister Harold Macmillan was telling folk they'd 'never had it so good'. It may not have seemed like that to everyone, but in essence he was not far wrong. Televisions, fridges, washing machines and cars were being bought at a rate unimaginable just a few years earlier. For once optimism was replacing pessimism; and with greater confidence in the future the local economy was growing daily as demand for its products grew.

This is not just a picture of a cottage or some simple stirring of the embers in any old firegrate. The old stools and fire irons in this room can tell a story going back over 200 years. In 1941 Mary Thornton was posing at the original grate in Wedgwood's Black Basalt Room. There had been a tour of the premises and she was demonstrating how the grate had been used in the days when Black Basalt was the company's most famous product. It was the first ornamental body that old Josiah Wedgwood had developed. He was quoted as saying, 'The Black is sterling and will last for ever.' He was not the first to produce a black body. Several earlier potters had developed one called 'Egyptian Black'. As with everything he did, Josiah was determined to turn out the best he possibly could. He put his heart and soul into developing a fine grained black stoneware that could be seen to match the Etruscan vases that were being uncovered in archaeological digs. He described his ware as being 'A fine black porcelain, having nearly the same properties as the basalts, resisting the attacks of acids; being a touchstone to copper, silver and gold and equal in hardness to agate or porphyry.' Josiah did not believe in using one word where several dozen would do! In 1768 Wedgwood developed a fine black porcelain known as black basalt, another innovation which proved to be a huge commercial success. The Wedgwood factory could hardly keep up with the demand for black basalt items. It was particularly popular with 18th Century ladies who loved the striking contrast of the black basalt and their fine white skin.

Goodwin PLC - Founding For the World

Goodwin PLC is one of the best known business names in Stoke-on-Trent. Local companies which fall within the Goodwin Group include Goodwin Steel Castings Ltd, Goodwin International Ltd, Easat Antennas Ltd and Dupré Minerals Ltd.

Goodwin Steel Castings Ltd

Based at the Ivy House Foundry, in Hanley, Goodwin Steel Castings Ltd. has been a supplier of machined castings since

1883 when the family firm first rented old colliery buildings on the site. Today, as part of Goodwin PLC, Goodwin Steel Castings Ltd is the foremost independent producer of high alloy and high quality integrity castings in the United Kingdom.

One of the ten oldest companies listed on the UK Stock Exchange, the firm of iron founders and engineers was established as a partnership led by Ralph Goodwin. Ralph's partners were his four sons, George, John, Ralph junior, and William, together with Fred Rushton and John Goodwin's own two sons: John Stanley, and Frank. Following return from active service in the First World War it was John Stanley Goodwin who became Chairman and Managing Director, working with his brother Frank.

During the hard times of the 1920s the business diversified into producing many articles, including brick-making machinery and tyre mould castings for Michelin. In 1926 profits had amounted to just £159. As a result of diversification profits had doubled by 1929 to £354!

John Stanley Goodwin retired in 1966, handing over the reins to his son, another John, who had already been in the business for twenty years.

In 1984 Goodwin's was the first steel foundry in the world to be awarded ISO9001 accreditation by the British Standards Institution, the company is also accredited to the 14001 Environmental and 18001 Health and Safety standards. Goodwin Steel Castings now has many years experience in manufacturing, machining and assembling castings for the steam turbine power generation industry.

A unique feature of Goodwin's is that it can supply fully assembled valves ready for delivery direct to the power station or the turbine manufacturer. Castings are produced in CrMo and CrMoV creep resistant steels, and in the improved performance 9.5CrMoWNbN steels for super and ultra-supercritical applications. The company also produces 'next generation' nickel-based super alloy castings for advanced pulverised coal-fired power plants. Casting at Goodwin's is not however limited to meeting the needs of industry. The struggle of the Shelton Bar steelworkers in the 1970s to retain their

livelihood has become an industrial folk-legend. Ted Smith, leader of Stoke Council headed the fight. A statue of a steel worker was used as a 'mascot' during marches around the streets. Sculptured by Colin Melbourne (head of the Sir Henry Doulton Sculpture School) in 1974, the Stainless Steel casting was produced at the Goodwin foundry. The statue portrays a

*Top: A very early view of the Goodwin factory (top right of centre of the picture) from the 1920s. **Above left:** A 1952 advert. **Left:** The casting is the tub of a 'beater' used for processing paper pulp as part of the paper manufacturing process. **Above:** The photo shows part of the Goodwin melt shop and shows molten steel being transported in a ladle, for transfer to the refining vessel. Goodwin are able to raise a total of 35,000kg for a single pour.*

steel worker dressed in traditional protective clothing. His helmet has a raised visor which opens to reveals the man's face; he holds a furnace lance in his hands. The plinth is a trapezoid shape, with inscribed plaque, itself standing on a brick pedestal. Colin Melbourne presented the sculpture to the Shelton Bar Action Committee. Sadly the fight was lost. After more than 100 years of continuous operation the blast furnaces were shut down in 1978 and 2,000 workers were made redundant. The whole works finally closed in 2000.

Today the statue stands outside the Potteries Museum and Art Gallery where it was installed in 1976. A plaque on the plinth reads:'I believe in the dignity of labour whether with head or hand; that the world owes no man a living, but that it owes every man an opportunity to make a living. This sculpture was created to commemorate the struggle of the Shelton Steel Workers to preserve the future of their works for the community.'

Though the firm of R Goodwin & Sons had been founded in 1883 R Goodwin & Sons (Engineers) Ltd was only incorporated in 1935. Today's holding company, Goodwin PLC, came into being in 1982. With the creation of Goodwin PLC came a coat of arms. Prepared by D.H.B. Chesshyre (Chester Herald of Arms) the firm's armorial bearings were awarded in 1983 – the 100th anniversary of its founding. The company may use the arms as long as the Goodwin family retains a controlling interest. The coat of arms is coloured black, red and gold. Black was chosen for its industrial connotations. Red and gold are the colours of molten metal, whilst gold is also a symbolic reference to the wealth generated by industry. Wings symbolise overseas interests. The mill rind in the centre of the wings is the heraldic symbol for an engineering connection. In heraldry, a mill-rind or Fer-de-Moline represents the iron which holds a millstone in place. Also featured in the coat of arms is a

Stafford Knot, a reminder that the Goodwin family and company were established in the county of Staffordshire. Oak leaves indicate the English roots of the family and company, the ivy leaf because the foundry is located in the ancient Ivy House Estate. On top of the of coat arms is a furnace man. In his hand he also holds a mill-rind. The motto or 'Mote' is 'On fonde pour le monde' – punning French for 'One founds for the world.'

John Goodwin who led the company for 23 years died in 1992. Faced with a catastrophic decline in the company's traditional markets in the coal and steel industries he had transformed the company's prospects by seeking out new products and new markets. John Walker Goodwin replaced his father as Chairman. Richard Stanley Goodwin became Managing Director.

Unsurprisingly for such an enterprising business Goodwin's has been given public recognition for its achievements. The Queen's Award for Enterprise is the UK's most prestigious award for business performance. In 2006 the Queen's Award for International Trade was awarded to Goodwin Steel Castings for its year on year increase in export sales - an increase mainly based on exports of fully-assembled stop and control valves for the power generating industry. Over 80% of the output was exported, mainly to the USA, India, China, Korea, and Japan.

Centre left: The Goodwin coat-of-arms. Top right: The steel worker statue which can be seen outside the Potteries Museum and Art Gallery. Left: Goodwin employees present at the award ceremony. Seated is Councilor Jean Edwards the Lord Mayor for Stoke-on-Trent for 2006-7. Above: The Lord-Lieutenant of Staffordshire presents the Queens Award on behalf of the Queen. Receiving the award are John Goodwin (Chairman Goodwin PLC) and Steven Birks (General Manager of Goodwin Steel Castings Ltd).

Goodwin International Ltd

Also within the Goodwin 'family' of businesses is Goodwin International Ltd. The company has the most modern and comprehensive machining company attached to any UK foundry and is based some five miles from the Goodwin foundry and has had ISO9001 accreditation since 1984.

Today the company is the market leader in the manufacture and design of Dual Plate Check Valves for use in the world's hydrocarbon, energy and process industries. With a track record of supply spanning almost 30 years the company has developed an enviable reputation for quality and reliability of product at competitive prices.

Based in Stoke-on-Trent, Goodwin International exports to over 50 countries. With some US$ 7,500,000 of inventory in 16 locations worldwide, the company offers outstanding support to its customers which include many of the world's largest oil companies and international engineering contractors.

Goodwin's engineering machining, fabrication and assembly capability is its key strength - enabling them to supply finish machined components to power generation, structural and nuclear facilities world wide.

Goodwin's first submersible pump units were installed for British Coal in 1981 at Cwm Washery in South Wales. Goodwin expanded the installations into British Steel and the Central Electricity Generating Board from 1983 onwards.

In 1996 Goodwin established a presence in Africa, installing submersible slurry pumps in applications for the gold, copper and platinum mining industries

In 2005 Goodwin to manufacture and sell the Goodwin submersible slurry pump worldwide.

Following the success of the Goodwin submersible slurry pumps in India, Goodwin PLC set up sales, manufacturing and servicing outlets for its pumps in China and Brazil in 2008.

Top left: Goodwin International's Submersible Slurry Pump, proven to succeed in the most demanding environments. **Above:** *Computer measurement of the pattern for the tower saddles on the Hardanger Suspension Bridge in Norway.* **Left:** *Assembly of a 600MW power station stop valve.*

machines. These ensure that only raw materials of the highest grades and quality are used in any of the Group's mixing facilities throughout the world. All 'Investment Powder' used in injection moulding produced must pass stringent test-criteria specifications before dispatch. Every batch of Investment Powder produced is tested in a full casting trial in the group's in-house casting shop.

Goodwin Refractory Services Ltd

Goodwin Refractory Services Ltd is one of the world's largest manufacturers of Block Moulding Industrial Investment Powder designed specifically for vacuum casting aluminium and other low-temperature, non-ferrous metals.

In recent years the automotive industry sector has grown significantly and the manufacture of turbo charger wheels has become an industry in its own right as all engine manufacturers look for increases in power and efficiency of their latest designs. Modern turbo chargers help improve fuel efficiency, economy and power, and reduce emissions throughout the operating range.

The extensive laboratories, sited in Newcastle-under-Lyme, are staffed with highly-trained technicians, and are equipped with state-of-the-art testing machinery, such as the XRF, XRD and thermal expansion

Only after passing these casting trials and showing no faults, is the batch of powder released to the customer.

A state-of-the-art, computer-controlled mixing plant and bagging facility, consisting of two five-tonne mixers, is also based in Newcastle-under-Lyme. This is the most modern Investment Powder manufacturing plant in the world and is the largest of its kind, capable of producing upwards of 2,000 tonnes per month of Investment Powder on a 24 hours a day, six days a week basis.

Top left and top right: *Examples of turbo charger wheels manufactured using GRS powders and used in the Bugatti Veyron, the worlds fastest production car.*
Left: *Goodwin Refractory Services Ltd's Gold Star furnaces ensure complete burnout occurs, preventing cool areas which will give incomplete burnout with carbon residues, and will adversely affect the quality of the final casting.*

Easat Antennas Ltd

Another Goodwin company, also with its base at Goodwin House, Leek Road, Hanley, is Easat Antennas Ltd. Easat was set up in 1987.

Easat designs and manufactures radar systems, installs and maintains complete surveillance radar sensor systems, or purpose designed radar antenna and radar turning units. These radars are used for surveillance of air, ground and sea targets for airport, port border security and military applications.

Since 1990, Easat has supplied radar equipment to over 40 countries world wide, spread over five continents. In an average year 90% of the company's sales and support activities are exported.

Amongst Easat's products is its Tactical Deployable Air Surveillance Antenna. This type of antenna can be supplied either trailer-mounted or palletised. The antenna system is self-contained and capable of being transported by ship, aeroplane, and helicopter, or by being towed to site. The design provides for rapid deployment in

less than 30 minutes from arrival at the operating location. Easat has designed a range of high-performance, low-cost Linear Array antennas specifically for Ground Movement Radar Control at airports.

The Easat Linear Array antenna EA6501 is targeted at the SMR markets in the USA. The model EA7401M is targeted at the SMR markets in other parts of the world such as Canada, Europe and the Pacific Basin.

This antenna is used at all major airports in Canada, and also at many major European airports such as Brussels, Zurich and London Heathrow.

Top left: *Eamples of Easat antennas.* **Above and below:** *The Easat range of antennas, pedestals and ancillary equipment is manufactured and tested in facilities audited to BS EN ISO 9001-2000.*

Dupré Minerals

Dupré Minerals was founded in the early 1950s. Based at Spencroft Road, Newcastle-under-Lyme, it manufactures an extensive range of high quality products, servicing the Vermiculite, Precision Casting, Friction and Refractory Industries. Dupré combines decades of experience with the latest production technology to formulate and manufacture the highest quality products to meet precise specifications.

Processing and manufacturing Vermiculite continues to be a core business. Vermiculite is a naturally occurring mineral that has applications wherever fire protection, absorption, and acoustic properties are desired. It is however the thermal insulation properties of Vermiculite that are most commonly sought and Vermiculite is an ideal user friendly option for domestic and industrial insulation applications.

The established Dupré brand inspired the development of some of the world's most advanced Vermiculite formulations. Applications for crude and exfoliated Vermiculites include insulation, friction, horticulture, construction and packaging. It is used wherever lightweight or heat resistant properties are required.

In 2007 Dupré opened a newly constructed Vermiculite exfoliation plant. This, in addition to the existing facility, provides a bulk storage capacity for over 5,000 tonnes of Vermiculite, safeguarding market supply and offering greater flexibility in service to customers.

The Dupré 'Micafil' brand is the market leader for insulation Vermiculite. Micafil is commonly used for a variety of building insulation applications, including internal cavity wall, loft and chimney flue liner. The Vermiculite operation also compliments the established range of Refractory, Precision Casting and Friction products

In 2009, Dupré started to provide Micalite Fire-Resistant Vermiculite Boards, ideal for use in wood-burning stoves and other insulation/fire resistance applications.

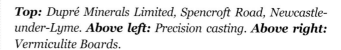

Top: *Dupré Minerals Limited, Spencroft Road, Newcastle-under-Lyme.* ***Above left:*** *Precision casting.* ***Above right:*** *Vermiculite Boards.*

Internet Central Ltd

As well as materials and engineering companies, one of the Goodwin PLC companies is Internet Central based at the Innovation Centre at Keele University. Internet Central is a specialist business internet and communications provider.

Today Goodwin PLC, now with some 17 companies within the Group, remains a family firm. It is not only one of the best known business names in Stoke-on-Trent but also a business with a reputation throughout the world.

THE WAR YEARS

Stoke-on-Trent was affected by a series of air raids during the war. Usually the bombers were seeking strategic targets such as the steel works, railway station and sewage works. Often the bombs missed and landed in residential areas such as this one in Pitts Hill and Old Stoke Road (p63), pictured the morning after the bombing raid in 1941. On the previous night the target was the Michelin tyre factory, with Stoke railway goods yard as a secondary target. At the time of the raids there was that feeling of helplessness that got to you. When the bombs fell, all you could do was take shelter and then hope and pray that your house was one of the lucky ones. Other significant targets included British Aluminium Works and Radway Green munitions factory.

During the Second World War the Central Bank was moved from London to Trentham Gardens as a precaution against bombing. The staff, mainly female, worked long hours here in very difficult conditions. The heating rarely worked, and many people worked with their overcoats on in winter. Whilst the ballroom at Trentham Gardens acted as a bank clearing house, the mail had to be sorted before it went any further. Outgoing communications passed through this area, as well. The foyer had never seen such activity. Tons of paper passed across its tiled floor as it was turned into the post office and paymaster general's section. The numbers on the wall in the picture top right were not put there to help the workforce choose the next hymn. They were there so that the women could accurately sort the mail into huge bags, before it was moved on to the next department or the outside world. Post Office Court in London was too vulnerable to attack from the bombing raids that the government knew would come. A direct hit could lead to complete confusion if important documents were destroyed in transit. Trentham Gardens had several advantages. Communication links were good. It was also not in an area

likely to be targeted by the Luftwaffe. In more peaceful times, the atmosphere at Trentham Ballroom could not have been more different. Trentham, as well as the King's Hall regularly took the opportunity to invite the well known big bands, mainly from the London area. Typical of these bands were the Ted Heath Orchestra, Joe Loss and his Orchestra and even Oscar Rabin. Everybody would enjoy these special occasions and the final song would almost always be "Who's taking you Home Tonight.'

The Lord Mayor, Lady Mayoress, Council Officials and Civil Defence members, seen below enjoying a warm drink from the tea van during the Second World War Mobile tea vans like this would have been operated by such groups as the Women's Voluntary Service to serve civil defence workers, policemen, firemen and soldiers who were undertaking tasks such as search and rescue after air raids.

Below: In 1939 Britain's Prime Minister Neville Chamberlain had made his announcement to the waiting people of Britain that '...this country is at war with Germany.' The country rolled up its sleeves and prepared for the inevitable. This war would be different from other wars. This time planes had the ability to fly further and carry a heavier load, and air raids were fully expected. Air raid shelters were obviously going to be needed, and shelters were built on open places across towns and cities. By the time war was declared an army of volunteers of both sexes

had already been recruited to form an Air Raid Protection service. It was their job to patrol specified areas, making sure that no chinks of light broke the blackout restrictions, checking the safety of local residents, being alert for gas attacks, air raids and unexploded bombs. The exceptional work done by Air Raid Wardens in dealing with incendiaries, giving first aid to the injured, helping to rescue victims from their bombed-out properties, clearing away rubble, and a thousand and one other tasks became legendary. Sir Anthony Eden, Secretary of State for War, appealed in a radio broadcast for men between 17 and 65 to make up a new force, the Local Defence Volunteers, to guard

vulnerable points from possible Nazi attack. Within a very short time the first men were putting their names down. At first the new force had to improvise; there were no weapons to spare and men had to rely on sticks, shotguns handed in by local people, and on sheer determination . Weapons and uniforms did not become available for several months. In July the Local Defence Volunteers was renamed the Home Guard, and by the following year were a force to be reckoned with. Other preparations were hastily made. Place names and other identifying marks were obliterated to confuse the enemy about exactly where they were. Notices went up everywhere giving good advice to citizens on a number of issues. 'Keep Mum - she's not so dumb' warned people to take care what kind of information they passed on, as the person they were speaking to could be an enemy.

Right, facing page: It was possibly the acute wartime shortages of food and supplies which made doctors, health workers and mothers alike very aware of the health of the new generation, and children were carefully weighed, measured and immunised against the illnesses that had at one time meant disfigurement or even death. A vaccine for polio, the scourge of former years which left behind its terrible mark of wasted and useless limbs, only came later, however. American scientist Jonas Edward Salk developed a vaccine in 1955, and an oral vaccine was produced in 1960. The vaccines brought the dreaded disease under control and today polio is rarely seen. On a day to day basis, vitamins were vital to the health of children, and long before the advent of the cod liver oil capsule, the recommended spoonful of cod liver oil was administered to the youngest children every day in schools and nurseries around the country during the 1940s. Children might have screwed up their noses at the fishy taste, but the nourishing cod liver oil went a long way towards keeping them healthy. The vitamin-packed orange juice was far more palatable, and artful mothers would often use the orange juice as a bribe: no cod liver oil, no orange juice. Following hard on the heels of the oil, the juice took away the distinctive taste that was disliked by so many children.

Right: Light tanks came rolling down Parliament Row, Hanley, in 1941. Happily, they were not Panzers. Those divisions had been the main thrust of the German invasion of Poland in 1939. The Netherlands, Belgium, Luxembourg and France in 1940 all heard the rumble of the caterpillar tracks as they fell under the

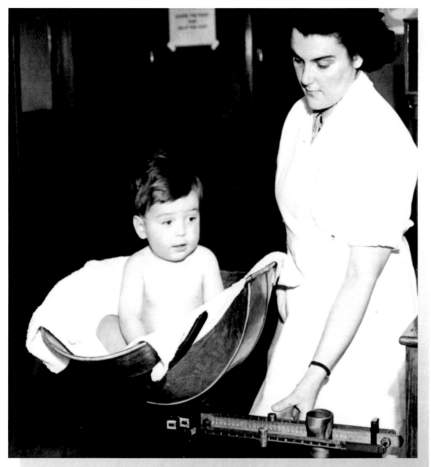

Nazi onslaught. In the campaign against France, there were 10 Panzer divisions involved. There were 2,574 German tanks in that campaign, out of the 3,400 tanks that Germany possessed. The cobblestones of the city centre shook as shoppers stood and watched the parade drive by. The army was on a morale and fund-raising exercise. Special tank, warship and aeroplane weeks were to become regular efforts in the 1940s. Rather than just ask for money, the government used the idea first tried successfully in the 1914-18 war. Towns and cities focused on raising funds for a single purpose. People could then identify with the aim. One week it would be funding for a battleship, the next for a Spitfire. That went down well with locals. Stoke-on-Trent's own Reginald Mitchell was the plane's designer. Towns were encouraged to compete with neighbours to see which ones would top the fund raising league table. Thermometers, charting the progress, appeared on town halls and in market places. Aluminium saucepans were handed in and reappeared flying through the skies, bearing the roundels of the RAF.

ROYAL VISITS

Workers wait in excited anticipation at one of the several pottery factories toured by King George and Queen Mary in April 1913.This was only two years after the Kingís coronation. At this time the pottery industry was suffering from foreign imports and imitations of prestige ware - Wedgwood and Doulton in particular. At one point during their visit it was reported that the Queen saw some Doulton figurines, and saw one called 'Bedtime'. She said "Oh, what a darling", and that little

figurine is still called 'Darling' as a result. A line of employees hold large platters with the message 'Your Majesties' Loyal Potters' painted on the platters. When their majesties came out, the plates had been turned over and they read 'God Save the King'. They toured several pottery factories on this day. They stayed at Crewe Hall, and their nest visit to the Potteries was important because, on that visit in 1925, the King created a city out of the County Borough of Stoke-on-Trent.

Princess Mary of Teck in the Kingdom of Württemberg had married her husband the Duke of York, the future King George V, in 1893. She had in fact been earlier engaged to his elder brother, Prince Albert the Prince of Wales and heir to the throne. Sadly Albert died six weeks later. In 1935, King George V and Queen Mary celebrated their silver jubilee, with celebrations taking place throughout the British Empire. In his jubilee speech George paid public tribute to his wife, having told his speechwriter, "Put that paragraph at the very end. I cannot trust myself to speak of the Queen when I think of all I owe her." Yet no wonder Queen Mary looks grim: her husband's health was failing fast, he had just twelve months to live. And then there was the problem of Edward, Prince of Wales, the Queen's eldest, and wayward, son. His biggest problem was that American woman Mrs Simpson. The following year would see the widowed Queen Mary become Queen Mother, and not one, but two, of her sons in turn ascend the throne.

Above: King George V and Queen Mary are pictured here with the Mayor of Newcastle, William Mellard, on the dais in Nelson Place, enjoying a civic welcome to the town. The King and Queen visited North Staffordshire on the 22nd and 23 April, 1913.

Below: All eyes are on this young lady at work at the Wedgwood factory in 1935. But she isn't taking her eyes off the job. She wouldn't dare – Queen Mary looks as if she eats young girls for breakfast. Even the Mayor is standing well back!Queen Mary, Queen Elizabeth's grandmother, had a reputation for being as stiff as her whalebone corsets. Her Serene Highness

Below and bottom right: In 1920 Burslem was in festive mood. The bunting was out to celebrate the visit by Edward Prince of Wales to the town. Here in the Market Place the old Town Hall, and Meat Market (demolished in 1958), formed the centre of the day's events. No one would have predicted that in the following years the immensely popular Edward would plunge the country into a constitutional crisis as a result of his wish to marry his long-time mistress the American Mrs Simpson. The old Town Hall, Burslem's second, was opened in 1857 to enormous acclaim. At the official opening a public dinner was prepared and served by Mrs Lees, the landlady of the Leopard Hotel across the way. As well as being Burslem's first concert venue, the Town Hall also provided offices for the new Town Council in 1878 when Thomas Hulme, a partner in MacIntyre

Pottery, became the first mayor. Burslem's famous coat of arms bearing the legend 'Ready' was incorporated at the same time. Atop the Town Hall clock tower can be seen the town's famous 'Gold Angel'. The angel was removed in February, 1998, whilst refurbishment work took place for the Ceramica project. The angel was on display in the Potteries Museum, Hanley, and then at the Royal Doulton Visitor, in Burslem. The angel was subsequently taken to the premises of Bailey International Steeplejacks in Macclesfield for restoration and re-gilding prior to repositioning.

Above: The Duke of Edinburgh visited Stoke-on-Trent on 12 December, 1951. The Guard of Honour in front of Stoke station was provided by the Stoke-on-Trent Sea Cadet Corps. Petty Officer Peter Wilkins (behind the officer of the guard) and leading seaman Bob Jenkins were from the former Stone Sub Division.

Above: The Second World War may have been over for fours years at the time this photo was taken, but the number of young women in uniform makes it seem like a wartime parade. The picture was taken on 2 November, 1949, when the then Princess Elizabeth visited Newcastle. Her Royal Highness is pictured here meeting WRACs from the North Staffordshire Regiment while soldiers on the right hold back the crowd eager to see the princess who, in only a few short years, was destined to be crowned Queen. Princess Elizabeth was no stranger to uniforms. In 1945, she had joined the Women's Auxiliary Territorial Service, as an honorary Second Subaltern with the service number of 230873. She trained as a driver and mechanic, drove a military truck, and was promoted to honorary Junior Commander. Among other locations in the area Princes Elizabeth also visited Enderley Mills on her tour of the town. At the time this photograph was taken the ever-popular Princess was still almost a newly-wed. She and Prince Phillip had married on 20 November, 1947.

Right: The year is 1973. The date is the 25th May. For once the sun is shining brightly as Her Majesty Queen Elizabeth II takes a walk along High Street. In front of Henry White's the Queen is collecting flowers proffered by her loyal subjects. The occasion is Newcastle's 'octocentenary' - a word we suspect was specially minted for the eight hundredth anniversary of the granting of the charter which first gave the town its borough status. Not in the picture, but not far behind, is Prince Philip, Duke of Edinburgh. As part of their visit the Royal couple later attended the Civic offices and Guildhall where Mayor Reginald Lane presented Her Majesty with a piece of local pottery to mark the event.

Right: When the King and Queen paid a wartime visit to Stoke-on-Trent it came as a complete surprise to everyone. Thousands would have turned out to cheer the royal couple had they known beforehand about the visit, but during the war strict security measures were needed to protect the nation's leaders. But word soon spread that the royal couple were in the area and they were warmly welcomed at Stoke Station. After a refreshing cup of tea obtained from the WVS mobile canteen the King and Queen watched a parade of Civil Defence Services in Station Square. They then visited Shelton Steelworks where they watched a blast furnace being tapped before going on to tour the Spode factory. During World War II King George and Queen Elizabeth lived and suffered with the people of Britain through the dark days of war. The royal couple showed great courage by staying on in England when they could have been evacuated to safety. They insisted that they be treated like everyone else, even to wartime rationing, and the King was almost relieved when Buckingham Palace was bombed. He felt that he could now identify with his people and look them in the face.

ENTERTAINMENT, LEISURE & PASTIMES

This page: Enoch Arnold Bennett (1867-1931) pictured above second left, in a family photograph was one of Stoke-on-Trent's greatest 'products'. An English Novelist and playwright he wrote many novels based on his hometown of Hanley and Stoke-on-Trent. Among his famous novels are Hannah of the Five Towns, The Card and A Man from the North. He preferred to work in solitude and spent many hours in quiet rooms alone awaiting inspiration. This room, pictured right, in a country house in Essex, was his favourite in England. Bennett's infancy was spent in genteel poverty, which gave way to prosperity as his father succeeded as a solicitor. After a local education Bennett finished his education at the University of London and for a time was editor of Woman magazine. His enduring fame is as a Chronicler of the Potteries towns, the setting and inspiration of some of his most famous and enduring literary work and the place where he grew up. His most famous works are the Clayhanger trilogy and The Old Wives' Tale. These books draw on his experience of life in the Potteries, as did most of his best work. In his novels the Potteries are referred to as "the Five Towns"; Bennett felt that the name was more euphonious than "the Six Towns" so Fenton was omitted. Many of the locations in Clayhanger and other Bennett novels are based in "The five towns" and correspond to actual locations in and around the Potteries district of North Staffordshire. He separated from his French wife in 1922 and fell in love with the actress Dorothy Cheston, with whom he stayed for the rest of his life. He died of typhoid at his home in Baker Street, London, on 27 March 1931, after returning from a visit to France. His ashes are buried in Burslem cemetery.

Above: What's this? A drunk being wheeled home in Hanley? Or perhaps these two chaps are having a joke at our expense. The style of dress, not least that top hat, suggests a very old photograph indeed. Photographers in the 19th century required their subjects to hold their poses sometimes for several minutes on end because of the slow process. That account's for the rather unhappy expressions on most Victorians' faces as they were told not to move a muscle until the photographer had finished. Perhaps though these gentlemen really are holding a pose – the gent on the barrow certainly looks to be holding a pocket watch in his left hand. Action snaps were impossible: movement just produced a blurred image. It seems unlikely however that this pair held their pose for more than a moment, indicating that the scene is from the early 20th rather than the 19th century. The records claim this picture is of a drunk being taken home from the old Roebuck Inn in Hanley, a long-gone local pub. The location however looks more like a builder's yard, with possibly the Roebuck Inn over the fence – the word 'Saloon' is just visible in an upper window.

This page: What a formidable-looking group. No wonder we won the war with women like these to stiffen our backbones. This photo was taken around 1938. The lady in the centre is believed to be the Mayoress of Stoke. Around her are former Mayoresses. Each of the ladies is wearing a medallion. Such Civic Awards measuring 80x54mm were presented to retiring Mayoresses to commemorate their service to the town. The 'jewel pendant' is made of gilt silver and coloured enamels with the arms of the city. Engraved on the reverse was the name of the recipient and the purpose of the award. Such awards are often treasured family heirlooms, though their commercial value is measured in hundreds not thousands of pounds. These Civic Awards were made locally, in Hanley. More surprisingly. similar awards, medals and livery badges were made in Hanley for the whole country. At the bottom of Market Square, Hanley, and by the junction with Fountain Square was H. Pidduck & Sons - the famous Hanley jewellers. Their shop first opened in 1841, was refurbished in the 1920s and rebuilt in the 1980s. In 1864 Henry Pidduck became the Mayor of Hanley. Perhaps it was his idea to start manufacturing medals for Aldermen and their wives. Although the Hanley branch of Pidduck's is now closed a branch in Southport, Merseyside. still trades today under the Henry Pidduck name.

This is not a scene from the Christmas panto 'Mother Goose', as you may think. It is however, the quite extraordinary scene from 1937 of Mrs Lockyer taking 'Billy' her pet goose out shopping in Stoke. Billy, from Shelton, was seen regularly out on the streets with his mistress, collecting large sums for charity. He had been taught by Mrs Lockyer to accept pennies in his basket. If geese are hand reared from goslings, with a significant amount of human contact, they become unafraid and friendly enough to eat from your hand. Billie was far more than just a pet and on occasions he would sit at the table and have afternoon tea with Mrs Lockyer.

The City Museum and Art Gallery was officially opened by Alderman Horace Barks on the 13th October, 1956. Built on the site of the Bell Pottery works, this image shows the area before additions were made to the building in the early 1980s. On the corner of Broad Street and George Street, now called Warner Street, is the Bell public house.

In the top left of the picture is the old water rates office, Bethesda Chapel, Bethesda Sunday school and the Victoria Hall. These buildings stand today outside the main entrance to The Potteries Museum and Art Gallery. As well as one of the largest and most important ceramics collection in the world, the museum also exhibits the Mark XVI Spitfire airplane, as a tribute to the

designer Reginald Joseph Mitchell (below), who was born in Kidsgrove in 1895. Mitchell completed the prototype Spitfire just a year before his death. The aeroplane was capable of 342 m.p.h. and was officially the fastest military aircraft of the time. This aircraft would be the basic design for the many marques of Spitfire that would help to win the air war for the Royal Air Force. Together with the Hawker Hurricane the Spitfire would be instumental in the Battle of Britain in the summer of 1940.

Below and top right: Here we are at Broom Street school in Hanley. The photographer has a captured a moment in the 1930s where some of the children are out at play on the climbing frame. Designed in the Queen Anne style by architect William Keates, the junior and infant school was completed in 1879 at a cost of £6,953. One of the larger schools of its kind, the building was intended to provide enough classroom space to accommodate up to 750 pupils. The Education Act of 1906 empowered local education authorities to provide free school meals. In 1921 this was extended to allow Authorities to provide free milk if they wished. About the time this photograph was taken an investigation by John Boyd Orr (published as Food, Health and Income in 1937) revealed that there was a link between malnutrition and under-achievement in schools. In 1946 Ellen Wilkinson became Minister of Education. She persuaded Parliament to pass the School Milk Act which ordered the issue of one-third of a pint of milk free to all pupils. The issue of milk continued until 1979 when Margaret Thatcher gained notoriety as Thatcher 'the milk-snatcher'. Pictured right, again

from Broom Street school, and dating from the 1950s are some junior boys enjoying their PE lessons. Or perhaps that should be 'PT' lessons. The difference between 'Physical Education' and 'Physical Training' may not have made much difference to what children actually did, but the change of name reflected changing attitudes. 'PT' implied training for war, 'PE' for peace.

Above: Crowds, mainly children, gathered at Longton Park during the holiday period waiting to use the paddling pool.

ere is Longton Park bowling green and one of its lakes. Officially the park's name is Queen's Park. The Queen was, of course, Queen Victoria. The public park was formally opened on 25 July, 1888, by George Granville William Sutherland Levison-Gower – the third Duke of Sutherland to those who prefer a shorter name. Longton Park is of course famous for its trees, horticulture and lakes. It has a very individual character and is one of the city's heritage parks. Today it houses a range of buildings including the clock tower and three bowling pavilions. This scene shows the park before the Second World War at a time when many of the trees were still only a few decades old. Each of the six towns had its

own municipal park and had competed to be the best. The park movement had begun in the mid 19th century in response to increasing urban overcrowding. Ordinary folk lived cheek by jowl in often terrible conditions. Wealthy philanthropists in every town and city caught the public park bug. In the second half of the 19th century hundreds of public parks appeared with band stands, lakes, gardens and scenic walks. For millions of people a walk in the park in ones Sunday Best clothes after church or chapel became a weekly ritual. The high point of the public park was undoubtedly the Edwardian era. The Second World War however witnessed a surge of use as the 'holiday at home' movement saw parks standing in the for the seaside.

Below: Hanley's Theatre Royal had a long and colourful history until its closure in 2000. In 1840 a disused Methodist Chapel on Brunswick Street was converted into a lecture hall by Thomas Hinde, and renamed 'the People's Theatre'. In 1871 a new 'Theatre Royal' was built on the same site but was destroyed by fire in 1949. It was rebuilt and reopened on 14 August, 1951. In 1961 it was sold to Mecca who operated it as a Bingo hall for twenty years. It reopened as a theatre in 1982, closed again in 1996, and was purchased by Mike Lloyd and refurbished in 1997. The curtain finally fell when Mike Lloyd's business empire collapsed in 2000. It was then converted into bars. Laurel and Hardy appeared at the Theatre Royal, Hanley, w/c 31 March 1952. Although both were suffering from poor health, they turned out good performances and apparently even managed a few tipples in the Mechanics' Inn, behind the theatre.

Below right: The Regent Theatre is a theatre in Stoke-on-Trent. It opened originally in 1929 as a super cinema and continued to be used as a cinema in various incarnations, originally as the Regent, under the ownership of Provincial Cinema Theatres, then as the Gaumont, and finally as the triple-screened Odeon, until its closure in 1989. Following a three year, £23 million development of the city centre, The Regent was reopened on 22 September 1999 after being fully restored to its previously elegant Art Deco style and has already been visited by a host of distinguished guests including Sir Derek Jacobi. Her Majesty the Queen officially opened The Regent Theatre in October 1999. The theatre holds 1600 patrons on two levels.

Wolverhampton's favour, which made them League Champions some time after the season had ended. Unfortunately, it was also the end of speedway racing at the Sun Street track as the stadium was sold for redevelopment. In 1973 a new stadium was built at Loomer Road, in Newcastle under Lyme and this continues to be home to Stoke. This resulted in them being known for one season as Chesterton Potters. A crowd of 6,500 watched Ole

The Stoke Potters team was formed in 1929 and speedway racing began at the Sun Street Stadium in Hanley. The Stadium had been built on a disused marl pit in order to host the first greyhound meeting in 1928. The speedway team were originally known as the Hanley Potters and attracted excited crowds of over 12,000. They later became the Stoke Potters when the five towns merged. After the second world war the Potters achieved success by winning the National League Division Three title and the 3rd Division National Trophy in the same 1949 season. After a closure in the 1950s the club enjoyed a successful spell in the early 60s after Mike Parker and Reg Fearman took over the reigns. The League Title was won on the track in 1963 by the "Stoke Potters" but was lost in the courtroom when Wolverhampton appealed to the Speedway Control Board over the inclusion of a rider who they claimed had not been registered correctly. The Court ruled in

Olsen cut the ceremonial tape before the first home meeting against Birmingham, while Ivan Mauger christened the track with a match race against former Stoke rider, Howard Cole, previously known as Kid Bodie. The sport has been ever present at Loomer Road since 1973, apart from one blank season in 1993 caused by financial problems and also in 1996 when the team merged with the recently closed Cradley Heath team to become the Cradley/Stoke Heathens. Normality returned in 1997 and the Stoke Potters are currently competing in the British Speedway Premier League.

Top left: 1953: Reg Fearman and Don Potter heading for a 5-1 over Leicester's Dennis Parker.

Left: Opening of the 1961 season: Pat Phoenix (Coronation Streets's Elsie Tanner) is introduced to the Stoke team by Reg Fearman.

Above: The crowning of Stoke Speedway Queen at the 1962 Stoke Speedway Dance.

Above: Does my bottom look big in this? This lass has all the potential for giving lads a tough time. Not only is she very pretty, but she also knows it. Look out, boys. She was obviously well aware of current fashion. Her modern, knitted two-piece was designed more to catch the eye than for practical purposes. The fabric would have got rather heavy and sag somewhat when immersed in the sea. Anyway, she was more interested in making waves among the males on the sands. The first modern two piece was created by Louis Réard in 1946, naming it the bikini after the atoll where atomic bomb tests were carried out. Réard reasoned that the costume's effects would be akin to that of a nuclear reaction and he was not far wrong. It blew some men's brains apart. However, more modest two piece costumes,

like the one seen here, had been modelled in the early 1940s by such movie stars as Ava Gardner, Lana Turner and Rita Hayworth. This lovely on the golden sands could dream that she was in the same league as those doyennes of the silver screen.

Top right: Once you had claimed your square yard of sand, that was it for the day, come hell, high water or the occasional rainstorm. Deckchairs were erected, albeit with some difficulty as the contraptions always seemed to have a knack of taking a chunk out of your fingers. The kids scrabbled around in the sand with their buckets and spades and mum smiled benignly and offered little bits of advice or warnings about making sure they knew where the family was if

they wandered off. The menfolk gazed out to sea passively, just happy that they had a week away from the shop floor. If the sun shone, those with flat caps were fine. They pulled them out of their pockets and plonked them squarely on their heads. It was the hatless ones who provided their own peculiar fashion statements. Whatever the temperature, the jacket stayed firmly in place, but the head was protected in a variety of ways. Some opted for the hankie, with a knot tied at each corner. Then there was the tea towel. Quite how this managed to get itself packed is a mystery, but it found its way onto the beach year after year. The newspaper made a good titfer. Either opened at the middle page and placed aloft or carefully crafted into a Robin Hood style by the use of South Yorkshire origami, it did its job.

Below: Coach trips were popular during the 1950s, and much quicker and more comfortable than the early charabancs. Here is a company's staff outing, probably from Royal Doulton, about to depart for Blackpool on May bank holiday 1958.

Right and below: The original Hanley Odeon was designed in the Art Deco architectural style for which the chain was famous, and was built on the site of the Grand Theatre, the legendary variety hall that was destroyed by fire in 1932. Not long after this image from 1959 was taken,there was to be an unhappy turning point for the silver screen, after the boom years of the 40s and 50s. Television and bingo combined to undermine the near-universal tradition of spending an evening at the pictures, admissions plummeted and it would be many years before a radically different kind of cinema enjoyed a belated renaissance. Big luxurious cinemas like the Odeon, which seated 1,300 and had dominated the corner of Trinity Street and Foundry Street since the 1930s, were to be phased out in favour of multiplexes with as many as 10 or a dozen screens. At the time though, films like 'South Pacific were still massive

box office hits. So popular was the Rodgers and Hammerstein musical, that the soundtrack album spent more time at Number 1 in the UK album chart than any other album, spending 115 weeks at the top in the late 50s and early 60s. It appeared for 70 consecutive weeks at the top of the chart and was Number 1 for the whole of 1959. When this cinema was closed in 1975 the Gaumont in Piccadilly, Hanley, was renamed as The Odeon.

Above: Here we see the rather bizarre sight of a Roman soldier walking casually up Piccadilly towards the town. The soldier is not one of Caesar's centurions but an employee of the Odeon cimema and is out and about drumming up business for the latest big screen blockbuster, the 1953 film 'The Robe'. Ten years in the making this Oscar-winning Biblical epic starring Richard Burton, Jean Simmons and Victor Mature told the story of a Roman military tribune who commands the unit that crucifies Jesus. The film was made by 20th Century Fox and is notable for being the first film released in the widescreen

process CinemaScope. A few months earlier in August 1953, a relative of RMS Titanic Commander, Captain E.J. Smith was invited to the showing of the "Titanic" film at the Odeon Cinema. Sarah Harris, who was 94 at the time, was the first cousin of Captain Smith and his only living relative, when she was specially invited to see the film. Edward John Smith was born in Hanley, Stoke-on-Trent, in 1850. He attended the Etruria British School until the age of 13 when he went to Liverpool to begin a seafaring career. He was the captain in command of the 'Titanic', and died on board when the ship sank in 1912. There is a statue to his legacy in Beacon Park, Lichfield. In the background are the old Boots Chemist and on the left is the familiar site at the time of a PMT rear entrance double-decker bus as it heads off to Kidsgrove. The company began life as Potteries Motor Traction Limited. It expanded beyond its Staffordshire base into Merseyside, Cheshire and Greater Manchester. The traditional colours of the PMT fleet were red and cream.

Below: A heated pool was built in the grounds of Trentham Hall, home of the Dukes of Sutherland. Trentham Hall was abandoned by the family as a permanent residence in 1905. In 1910 the Duke offered the hall to the County of Staffordshire and the Borough of Stoke-on-Trent. The offer was refused and the building was demolished, apart from the west front and stable block. The grounds were opened to the public, and today have been developed as an exhibition, conference and leisure centre. The pool has now been filled in.

Right: The Palace, Albion Street, which opened on Boxing Day 1932, was another of Hanley's enormous 'pleasuredomes'. With 2,000 seats all on one level and a 30ft-wide screen, it was thought at the time to be the largest in Staffordshire. Built in 1907 it had an interesting history and several different owners, originally starting life as a wooden roller skating rink. Multi-use events such as boxing and dances continued until it closed in 1930. Two years later, after extensive renovations the building was reopened as The

Palace cinema. This was an ideal venue to see one of the biggest screen stars of all time, 'King Kong'. Canadian-born, Fay Wray was Kong's co-star and the film made approximately $2 million in its initial release, a massive amount in 1933. The Palace was taken over by the Newcastle based Essoldo Cinemas chain in August 1954 and re-named Essoldo. The Essoldo Cinema closed on 16 April, 1966, with Sean Connery in "Thunderball". It then spent many years as a bingo hall, first as Essoldo Big Bingo and finally as the Mecca Bingo Club, which closed on 22 April, 1998. The war memorial stands opposite Hanley Town Hall at the top of Albion Street. The memorial was unveiled on 11 November, 1922, by Mrs Cecil Wedgwood, JP. The inscriptions front and back read: 'To our valiant dead 1914 -1918. 1939 -1945' and 'They died for our freedom' There is a plaque inside the entrance to Hanley Town Hall inscribed with the names of fallen soldiers .

Above: City centre half Neil Franklin enjoys a cup of tea before leaving for the ground on match day. Widely considered to be the best centre half in Britain at the time, strong in the air, he tacked with great timing and showed great guile and intelligence when passing the ball. Cornelius (Neil) Franklin was born in Shelton on 24 January, 1922. He joined Stoke City in January, 1939. The team included players such as Stanley Matthews and Freddie Steele. Franklin's career was interrupted by the Second World War. He joined the Royal Air Force but as he was based in Blackpool he was able to continue to play football and made 186 appearances for Stoke City in friendly and regional fixtures as well as representing England in 10 wartime internationals. When peacetime soccer resumed he went on to make 142 League and 20 FA Cup appearances for Stoke, as well as winning 27 full England caps. By 1950, however, he was ready to leave Stoke - he was unhappy with the £20 a week maximum wage limit imposed by the FA, and he wanted to move his family away to a cleaner climate. Franklin sensationally hit the headlines when he headed off for Columbia having accepted a contract to play for the Santa Fe club in Bogota. Unfortunately things did not work out and Franklin and his family returned to Britain after just 4 weeks. A suspension from league football followed and he never played for Stoke or England again. In February, 1951, he moved to Second Division club Hull City for £22,500, at the time a world record fee for a defender. After leaving Hull, he had brief spells with Crewe Alexandra, Stockport County and Macclesfield Town.

Left: Stoke captain Neil Franklin shakes hands with Manchester City goalkeeper Frank Swift, in front of an enthusiastic Victoria Ground crowd, on New Year's Day, 1949. Stoke unfortunately lost the game 3-2. The Stoke goals were scored by Frank Bowyer, who ended the season as top goalscorer with 21, and legendary City striker Freddie Steele, who joined Mansfield Town after sixteen years at the Victoria Ground. In an inconsistent season Stoke finished mid-table, which was quite an achievement from a team with most players coming from the local area and which reportedly cost a mere £10 to assemble.

Bottom left, facing page: Is this one of the greatest gatherings of footballing talent ever to appear on the same pitch? The best footballers from across the world coming together to play in Stoke-on-Trent for the benefit of one man.... Sir Stanley Matthews! His testimonial took place at Stoke City's Victoria Ground on 28 April, 1965, some 33 years after the winger made his debut. The match was between Stan's XI and a World Stars XI, with some of the greatest players in the history of the game playing that night - Moore, Armfield, Cohen, Wilson, Hunt. Greaves and Charlton from the 1966 World Cup squad, plus the likes of Law, Puskas, Di Stefano, Eusebio and Lev Yashin between the sticks. Stoke won a thrilling, open and attacking game of football 6-4 and as the whistle blew for full-time Sir

Stanley is pictured being chaired off the pitch by World Stars Lev Yashin and Ferenc Puskas as Josef Masopust leads the applause for the 'Wizard of Dribble' off the pitch for the last time.

Above and below: Gordon Banks was born in Sheffield on 30 December, 1937. He played as goalkeeper for Stoke City F.C. between 1967 and 1972. They won League Cup in 1972 with a 2-1 victory against Chelsea. Afterwards

they toured the city in an open-topped double-decker bus. Banks was one of the greatest goalkeepers of his or any other generation and he will forever be remembered for his heroic part in England's triumphant 1966 World Cup campaign that culminated in the famous 4-2 victory over West Germany, at Wembley, in the final. Four years later, he was still England's number one as they headed to Mexico to defend their World Cup crown and produced the competition's most iconic moment when he spectacularly kept out Pele's header in the clash with Brazil in Guadalajara, a breathtaking effort which became known as the 'Save of the Century'. This was not just by chance as he was a glutton for training. Banks often asked his England team-mates to stay behind to take shots at him. Capped 73 times by his country, he finally hung up his gloves in 1972 at the age of 34 and is universally acknowledged as the first of what was to become a golden era of English goalkeepers. Banks also enjoyed a glittering club career that spanned three different decades, playing for Leicester City for eight years before spending five seasons with Stoke, during which time he played 246 senior games. He was awarded the OBE in 1970 and was named the Football Writers' Player of the Year in 1972.

Below: A very happy group of Port Vale supporters arrive at Euston Station, London, en route to watch their team play against Fulham in an FA Cup tie on 1 January, 1962. They had to squeeze into a massive crowd that packed Craven Cottage to see the exciting 5th round game. Port Vale fought gallantly but lost to a second half penalty, 4 minutes from time, from Fulham defender Langley. Fulham went on to lose 2-1 to Burnley in the semi-final replay.

Bottom right: The old Port Vale ground dominates this hilltop view of industrial Hanley, with its many pot banks and the spoil heap on the horizon - a very different place back in 1950 when this photograph was taken to the city we are familiar with today. Over the years the club saw a number of name changes; it was formed in 1876 as Port Vale Football club, and on moving to Burslem in 1884 Burslem Port Vale. They moved to the recreation ground in Hanley in 1913, dropping 'Burslem' from their name. Port Vale have fought their way through many difficult periods in their long history, but to their credit have always bounced back. Relegated for the first time in 1928-29, the Club responded by winning the Third Division (North) Championship, attaining 5th place in Division Two (still the Club's highest league position). Between 1936 and 1953 the club fluctuated between Third Divisions North and South. Port Vale left Hanley in 1950 for their present ground at Vale Park in Burslem, leaving the old stands at Hanley to the demolition teams.

Right: Possibly the most successful times for Port Vale have been in the 1950s. Vale Park was completed in 1950, the club's second ground, a year later Freddie Steele became manager. Steele quickly established himself at the club, masterminding the celebrated 'Iron Curtain' defence. The 1953-54 saw Vale storming to the Third Division North title as well as reaching the semi-finals of the FA Cup, losing out to eventual winners West Brom in very controversial fashion, seeing an Albert Leake goal disallowed for offside. The following year they lost out 4-2 in an exciting F.A. Cup 4th Round tie against Spurs. In the action right: Tottenham Hotspur's Johnny Brooks (l) fires a shot at goal as Port Vale's Reg Potts (third r), Roy Sproson (second r) and goalkeeper Ray King (r) try to block as Tottenham's John Gavin (No 7) looks on.

Below: Looking a little windswept these girls are taking a carefree stroll along the towpath of the Trent and Mersey Canal in 1939 . A stiff wind is whipping up the waters. Soon it will blow the storm clouds of war across the horizon. Children had walked this path for years. With their smart socks and frocks they dressed like little girls ought. They did not need to ape the pouting models and pop stars that make this century's kids old before their time. A bracing walk away from the smoking factory was the sort of entertainment that the modern Miss would sniff at. Jolly bargees would wave and smile as they made their way from Runcorn, through Burslem and on to the River Trent. The brightly decorated barges with their hand painted pots and jugs were a feature of the canal. Children loved to see them negotiating the locks. The water rushing in and out, through the paddle gates, was a wonder of engineering that fascinated them. There was plenty of opportunity to see them. The canal rose and fell through a series of 75 such steps.

Top right: This picture is the Empire Bingo Hall in 1967. Originally built as the Queen's Theatre in 1887, the building was destroyed by fire on 28 September, 1894. A new Queen's Theatre was built on the site, designed by noted theatre architect Frank Matcham and it opened in 1896. In 1916 it was re-named Empire Theatre and in late 1921 conversion was begun to cinema use, when a projection box was built into the roof of the building. It re-opened on 23 January, 1922 with some stage shows taking place, but film use became more prevalent and right up to closure it was always named the Empire Theatre. Taken over by the Regent circuit in 1925, they later became part of Associated British Cinemas (ABC). The building was given a Grade II Listed status and bingo continued until 1991 when it was operated by Gala Bingo Clubs. Sadly, a fire on New Year's Eve, 1992, destroyed the building. It was subsequently demolished in Spring, 1997. The importance of cinema as a social activity, as well as a cultural experience, for children at this time cannot be over-emphasised. This was an age before television, which wasn't available in the Midlands until 1949. Cinema-going was a habitual activity from the 1930s to the 1950s and the children's clubs were designed to nurture the habit from an early age. You could escape from your parents for a few hours on a Saturday morning and become part of the ABC Minors gang for about sixpence a week. A warm and cherished memory fifty, sixty or even seventy years later.

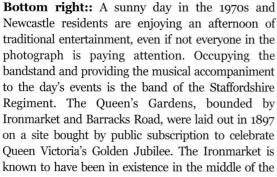

Bottom right:: A sunny day in the 1970s and Newcastle residents are enjoying an afternoon of traditional entertainment, even if not everyone in the photograph is paying attention. Occupying the bandstand and providing the musical accompaniment to the day's events is the band of the Staffordshire Regiment. The Queen's Gardens, bounded by Ironmarket and Barracks Road, were laid out in 1897 on a site bought by public subscription to celebrate Queen Victoria's Golden Jubilee. The Ironmarket is known to have been in existence in the middle of the 14th century. At the eastern end of Ironmarket was marshland, and an area of water called Colleswaynes Lake. Known as 'The Marsh' the waste land was owned by the borough. In 1782 The Marsh consisted of 23 acres. As early as 1698 the borough council had attempted to have The Marsh 'inclosed' but it was not until 1782 that an Inclosure Act was obtained. The first steps were taken to reclaim The Marsh by enclosing the site then described as being in a 'ruinous state'. The waterlogged area at the eastern end of the Ironmarket was soon drained to become Nelson Place, from which new streets radiated eastwards and southwards. Queen Street, King Street, and Brunswick Street were to the east, and on the south Bagnall Street, now Barracks Road. By 1818 all these streets were in existence. It would however be another 70 years before more money was forthcoming to complete the project and turn the last empty space into the Queen's Gardens.

The giant steel works at Shelton during its heyday. After the war Shelton was at full capacity and employed thousands of men, producing some of the finest steel in the world. Coal fed the huge blast furnaces, and these would light up the sky at night like a sunset. The site was cleared in 1986 and played host to the National Garden Festival in that year. The 1986 Stoke-on-Trent Garden Festival led to the reclamation of large areas of land west of the city centre area – including the former Shelton steelworks, which had been derelict since 1978. Ironically, when the Garden Festival closed, the land remained derelict for some time, before being re-developed into public parkland and for retail and leisure.

AROUND THE SHOPS

The Co-op Movement had its roots in Brighton where a local reformer, Dr William King, advocated the principles of self-help trading in home produced goods. In 1844 a group of Rochdale textile workers set up an independent business encouraging cooperation and providing the customer with a dividend on each purchased item, the accumulation of which went into shared profit. The birth of the Co-operative movement in Burslem can be traced back to 1901, with number 10, Newcastle Street being its first retail outlet. Burslem potter, James Colclough opened Stoke-on-Trent's first co-operative store. Local people had a life long interaction with the Co-op throughout

the 20th century. Initially you could buy your groceries like potatoes, flour, tea, sugar and butter which would be weighed out and wrapped in the shop, as you waited. As the 20th century progressed the Co-op provided everything you would ever need, from baby prams to beds and from TV's to hi-fi's. All eventualities are catered for, even funeralcare, when we are no longer around to appreciate the benefits.

The Co-op opened its dairy on Shelton New Road in 1929. It had its own body shop. Vehicles were customised from transporting meat into being milk floats. The brand spanking new Model A Fords shone brightly in the sunshine. They

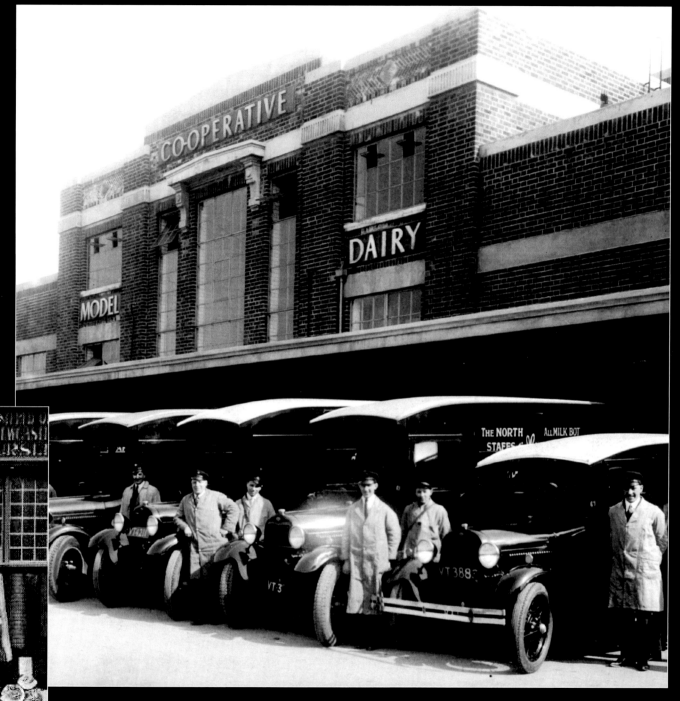

replaced the horse drawn vehicles that had previously trundled around the streets. A lot of the business was taken up in supplying milk to local schools. Every morning playtime, children in the primary school tucked into a third of a pint of good nourishment. After the Second World War every local authority had to provide free milk to schools. It was a way of improving the health of the nation's youngsters. Every morning they sat cross legged in a circle in front of the teacher. The straw monitor handed round the little cardboard tubes used to suck up the goodness. There always was one little monster, usually a boy, who blew bubbles. He was promptly scolded. It was a daily ritual. Straws and bottle tops were never thrown away. Another monitor collected them. They were given to the washing monitor for cleaning. Later that day they reappeared in the art and craft lesson. When Margaret Thatcher became Minister of Education in the early 1970s, free milk was taken away from schools. She was called 'Thatcher the milk snatcher'. The little bottles made a comeback in the 1980s, but many authorities made a charge for the service.

Above: Taken in 1932, this was the view looking down the Ironmarket from its junction with the High Street in Newcastle. To the left of the picture shop fronts with canopies stretch down to the Municipal Hall and then beyond to Nelson Place. To the right the pavement in the foreground is populated by shoppers and a row of parked cars can be seen pulled up to the curb. Mason's the cabinet maker is on the far left of the Ironmarket, with D. Read, the grocers, next door. The Municipal Hall was built between 1888 and 1890, to commemorate the Golden

Jubilee of Queen Victoria. During its time the Hall contained a Council Chamber, Library, Dance Hall, and School of Art. It was demolished in 1967 and the present Newcastle Library now occupies the site. Tram lines are visible running down the Ironmarket as at the time tram services ran from Newcastle to Burslem, Chesterton, Hanley, Silverdale, and Wolstanton.

Bottom left, facin page: Parliament Row runs from the Market Square at the top to Parliament Square and Old Hall Street at the bottom. This view is looking towards Town Road (was High Street) in the 1950s. This area is now pedestrianised. Near to where the lamppost is there now stands a statue of Sir Stanley Matthews. Woolworth's occupied the same store until their closure in December 2008. Swinertons cafe and the shops surrounding it have been replaced by the modern "Potteries Shopping Centre".

Left and below: This scene shows a billposter outside Woolworth's around the late fifties or early sixties. The poster advertises 'Subway in the Sky', which was showing at the Odeon cinema. The film released in 1959, starred Van Johnson and Hildegard Knef. It is hard to imagine the High Street without Woolworth's, but that is now the case. All 13 Woolworths branches in North Staffordshire, South Cheshire and Shropshire were set to close, in a 10-day period, at the end of 2008.

Below: Crikey! What are all these folk in Tunstall queuing up for? This is Tunstall's Tower Square. The date is the early 1950s. People are queuing patiently outside Naylor's Bon Marché. Word has gone round that something special is happening. The answer to the mystery is that some 'rare' item is now in stock. Though rationing was introduced during the Second World War to ensure the fair distribution of food and other items peace in 1945 did not signal the end of rationing. Many things were in short supply. Food rationing began in January 1940, four months after the outbreak of the war. At first limits were imposed only on the sale of bacon, butter and sugar. By March, 1940 all meat was being rationed. Before long clothes coupons were introduced. Inevitably a black market soon developed. Queuing outside shops and bartering for extra food became a way of life. Extra allowances were granted to pregnant women who used special green ration books to get additional food rations, whilst breastfeeding mothers were entitled to extra milk. Not until three years after the end of the war did restrictions begin to be lifted. Flour came 'off ration' on 25 July, 1948, followed by clothes in March the following year. Rationing ended for canned and dried fruit, chocolate biscuits, treacle, syrup, jellies and mincemeat in 1950. Three years later sales of sugar came off ration. Meat, the first to be affected, was also last; meat rationing ended only in July, 1954.

Above: St John's Square, Burlsem, on a quiet day in 1955. The old fashioned signpost directs motorists left to Hanley and Stoke; to the right is the road to Wolstanton and Newcastle. In those days the writing on signs was so small motorists often needed to stop to read them. The traffic authorities still thought in terms of horses and carts and hadn't quite got it into their heads yet that faster speeds meant less time to read. The black and white stripes on the signpost, and on the bollard too, are a reminder of earlier times. St John's Square may be well supplied with electric street lighting in 1955, but until ten years earlier Britain had been under a blackout.

To help folk get around a little better in the darkness white painted lines which had been in use before the war now appeared everywhere: on kerbs, stone steps, road markings and street 'furniture'. To a present generation used to powerful street lighting it is difficult to imagine how dark the nights could be even after the blackout ended. Major roads might have reasonably good electric lighting but gas lights were still commonplace until the 1960s. And it was not just ordinary darkness the lights had to contend with; in the days before we went 'smokeless' thick smog would all too often cover the Potteries.

Above: This 1960 photograph of the old Lewis's building in Hanley will no doubt bring back memories for the city's shoppers. The building was part of a complex which included Lewis's Arcade, a shopping mall built in the 1930s between Stafford Street and Lamb Street, Hanley. In 1963 Lewis's built new premises to replace their nearby store. When it opened it was the city centres largest shop. A 1967 Christmas window display full of toys at Lewis's department store, with no electronic video games or Playstations, but all low-tech toys such as dolls, books and jigsaws. This was one of a number of different themed windows which looked magical from the outside. Many readers will remember visiting Santa's Grotto in the hope of receiving a special Christmas present from the large man in the red outfit and white beard. The store was later integrated into the £45 million Potteries Shopping Centre which opened in June, 1988. The store was taken over by Owen and Owen, closed in September, 1998, and then reopened as Debenhams.

Right: It's market day in Hanley's Market Square. The year is 1960. On the left the large building is home to Swynerton's Café and Sherwin's music shop. The building was demolished in 1980 to make way for the Potteries Shopping Centre. In the background can be seen the Angel Hotel and The Grapes with its advert for 'Bass only'. The Angel Restaurant and Wine Store 'a handsomely fitted up establishment, where luncheons, dinners, suppers and all refreshments are served in first-class style' was built in the 1890s. Part of the Angel Vaults is still standing today and is used by The Abbey National

Building Society. Alfred Chew and Co, which owned the Angel restaurant and had its head office there, was founded in Hanley in 1887. Scotch whisky sold for 21 shillings per gallon and cigars at 42 shillings per dozen. By the time this photo was taken more than six decades later the price of whisky and cigars was a good deal higher. Yet despite price rises this was a period of ever-increasing affluence and optimism. Post war austerity was giving way to a new found prosperity. The Angel and The Grapes in Town Road (formerly High Street) had been replaced in part by a branch of the Abbey National and Halfords. More recently the Halfords site had been replace by the Co-operative Bank.

Above: A busy street scene outside the entrance to Hanley indoor market in the 1970's. Many readers will remember Goodwins the bakers, Swynerton's Café and Sherwins popular music store on the corner of Market Square. There has been a market in Hanley since the early 1600's, though it was 1791 before the then Lord of the Manor, John Bagnall, granted a 200-year lease to allow a market hall to be built. This early market was replaced by a much larger building in 1849. The current Hanley market still stands on the site of the 1849 general market as part of the Potteries Shopping Centre. This current market opened in November 1987 and houses 130 stalls, selling everything for the family and home,

not forgetting Stoke-on-Trent's delicious delicacies of oatcakes and pikelets.

Bottom left, facing page: Plans to reorganise Hanley's Market Square were being considered in the mid 1960's. And soon many well known and popular retail names would be gone forever – Huntbach's, Swinnertons', Sherwin's and McIlroy's, to name but a few. By the end of the 1970's the Angel and the Grapes were no more, replaced at first by Redman's butchers and then the new building of Abbey Bank and Halfords. The picture below shows scaffolding being erected in the 80's as work starts on the demolition of the market square stores and market hall, to make way for the Potteries shopping centre which opened in 1988.

Below: Here's a view of Newcastle High Street in the mid-1970s. Traffic appears relatively quiet despite the fact that vehicles do not yet have access to a better route. Perhaps the rain has made many drivers stop at home, though plenty have come to town and parked their cars to do some shopping. The 1970s coincided with a mania for giving listed status for older buildings, no doubt in response to the mania in the 1960 for tearing similar buildings down in the name of 'progress' and 'modernisation'. As a result of that reaction against modern architecture many of the buildings in High Street were saved for posterity by becoming classified as Grade II listed buildings. On the far right hand side of the picture is the Guildhall. A guildhall, presumably in High Street, existed at the end of the 13th century and the street itself is definitely mentioned in 1326. Over the rooftops can be seen the top of St Gile's church tower. The current church is largely Victorian in origin and was designed by Sir George Gilbert Scott. The beautiful interior provides a breathtaking space for worship or quiet reflection and prayer. Henry, Earl of Huntingdon, passed through Newcastle in 1663 and noted it as 'a long town, the High Street very broad, ill paved and houses poorly thatched and very few either tiled or slated'. He described the Guildhall as 'a fair reasonable town house', but the church, as it was then, 'neither fair nor handsome.'

WORKING LIFE

Below: Florence Colliery in 1969. North Staffordshire was a centre for coal mining. The first reports of coal mining in the area come from the 13th century. Part of the North Staffordshire Coalfield, the Potteries Coalfield covers 100 square miles (300 km2). On nationalisation of the industry in 1947, around 20,000 men worked in the industry in Stoke on Trent. Notable Collieries included Hanley Deep Pit, Trentham Superpit (formerly Hem Heath and Florence Collieries), Fenton Glebe, Silverdale, Chatterley Whitfield and Wolstanton The industry developed greatly and even new investments in mining projects were planned within the City boundaries as recently as the 1990s. However, 1994 saw the last pit to close as the Trentham Superpit was shut. The Stoke mining industry set several national and international records. Wolstanton Colliery, when modernised had the deepest mining shafts in Europe. In 1933, Chatterley Whitfield Colliery became the first Colliery in the country to mine 1 million tons of coal. In the 1980s Florence Colliery in Longton repeatedly set regional and national production records and in 1992 the combined Trentham Superpit (Hem Heath and Florence) was the first Mine in Europe to produce 2.5 million saleable tonnes of coal.

Left: Paintresses in their 'pinnies' working on Royal Doulton Character and relief-moulded jugs, 1947.

Below: A unique look inside a biscuit kiln as worker stack saggers. Row upon row of saggers have been piled high and even more are being added. The process of stacking the saggers was called 'settling in'. Hundreds of containers, filled with thousands of items, would be baked in a single firing.

Moorcroft
Fine Art Pottery

Tucked away behind Cobridge Park is a picturesque factory which makes fine art pottery. Along one boundary, a visitor will find a walkway which was once a rail loopline from Etruria to Kidsgrove. A bowler-hatted William Moorcroft would have stepped off the train at Cobridge Station, walked through a wrought-iron gate and into the new factory which still houses the company he founded and which proudly carries his name to this day. The factory was built in 1913, initially with a single bottle oven. A further two were added in 1915 and 1919, and two more in 1919/1920, of the final two, one was to fire flambé ware and the other to fire lustre ware. Only the large 1919 bottle oven survives to this day, itself a Grade II Listed Building of 'Outstanding Architectural and Historic Merit'.

The factory belongs to W Moorcroft PLC – or more simply 'Moorcroft'. The firm was founded a century ago by William Moorcroft.

Today, thanks to designs from the world-famous Moorcroft Design Studio and the consummate skills of a dedicated workforce, Moorcroft pottery enjoys unprecedented popularity and esteem.

The Moorcroft story started in 1897 in the heart of a large Burslem ceramic company, James Macintyre & Co Limited. There a twenty-four year old designer called William Moorcroft was bursting with ambition beyond his social standing - at a time when it was hard to find work, let alone secure a position which would enable him to design fine art pottery.

Good luck, in the form of a Methodist Sunday School in Burslem, the 'Mother Town of The Potteries', introduced William to the Woodall family who were the prosperous owners of James Macintyre & Co Limited. Macintyres manufactured porcelain insulators and switchgear - hardly a fertile home for young William's ambitious plans.

Fortunately for William it had become fashionable for major industrial manufacturers in the Potteries to produce their own art pottery as well as their usual bread-and-butter commercial and industrial lines such as drainpipes, bathroom-ware and domestic and hospitality transfer-printed earthenware and china.

Macintyres had already started down the road to diversification, and had appointed a well-known ceramic designer, Harry Barnard, from London. Fortunately, the Woodall family had a reputation for cultivating local talent, and their new recruit, William Moorcroft, was initially given the task of preparing transfer prints for his first design called Aurelian Ware. Even so, although the designs were his own, they were transfer-printed and

Top left: Founder, William Moorcroft. *Left:* Workers at the factory in the early years of the 20th century. *Top right:* The Moorcroft factory in the 1930's with its original five bottle ovens. *Above right:* 'Potteries in Recession' by Kerry Goodwin. This design was described by BBC Antiques Roadshow expert, Eric Knowles, as 'astoundingly brilliant'.

Initially only cobalt blue was available, and this Moorcroft applied in various shades of intensity to create 'blue-on-blue' ware. Under the skilled hand of Moorcroft, 'blue-on-blue' pottery mutated into what was subsequently called Florianware. This was the name of the design style which established William Moorcroft as a world-class designer. It was launched in 1898, and represented a blend between contemporary Art Nouveau and the decorative traditions of William Morris and the Arts and Crafts movement.

Moorcroft created many different Florian patterns, the majority based on English flowers – poppies, violets, tulips, irises, cornflowers, daisies and roses. Success was immediate.

transfer printing did not make fine art pottery. William knew it. To avoid any blemish to his future reputation, the young potter did not sign Aurelian Ware pieces, preferring instead to harness the techniques which Harry Barnard had initiated in his own work. Inevitably, artistic conflict between Barnard and Moorcroft followed. Surprisingly William Moorcroft won, and Barnard left to pursue a successful design career with Wedgwood. The ambitious young designer and ceramic chemist, schooled in the traditions of The Potteries, was now on his own.

William personally signed every piece of Florian ware which Macintyres made as a mark of his approval of its quality. Whilst the blue-on-blue designs became less prominent, other new and more vibrant colours emerged. First came yellows and greens, followed by reds, orange and purple. The use of metallic oxide colours enabled a new star to enter the ceramic firmament and in 1904, Moorcroft won a gold medal at the St. Louis International Exhibition in the United States.

The departure of Harry Barnard was a heaven-sent opportunity for young William. Tubelined designs in-filled with metallic oxide colours followed one another in quick succession.

Although the idea of introducing the seventeenth century art of tubelining had originated from Barnard, decorating with metallic oxide colours was a totally original idea from the young potter who was also a chemist.

Top left: The Liberty Tea Rooms featuring the Moorcroft **'Powder Blue'** teaset, circa 1930's. **Centre left:** Florian ware **'Poppy'** design, circa 1900. **Centre right:** **'Spirit of Liberty'** 2002, by Emma Bossons, FRSA. **Below:** Girls at work in the Moorcroft decorating room in the 1950s.

That walk must have been a sight to remember. Casters, turners, tubeliners and painters, all walking crocodile-style, one after another carrying their paint brushes, tubeliners' squeezy bags, tools and equipment.

The journey was re-enacted after the Moorcroft centenary in 1997, with one-hundred and three-year-old Pattie Booth, leading the way in a wheelchair pushed by the then Arts Minister, Richard Caborn. Pattie Booth (nee Machin) was eighteen years old when she first carried her paint brushes and bowls across the park in 1913.

The move to the new factory saw an outpouring of glorious new designs. The iconic Pomegranate design was finalised, and the famous Spanish Pattern made its first appearance. It was not long before the Arts and Crafts style Cornflower pieces emerged from the Moorcroft bottle ovens.

Stores such as Tiffany & Co in New York and Shreve and Co. in San Francisco started to retail Moorcroft pottery, and by so doing, joined the illustrious company of Liberty & Co., of Regent Street, London. The opening of an account with Liberty & Co. was a defining moment for Moorcroft. Arthur Lazenby Liberty had been a friend and mentor of the young ceramic designer, both in personal and in family terms, so much so that on the death of his first wife, Florence, (nee Lovibond), William married Hazel, a member of the Liberty family.

Back in Burslem however, William's relationship with James Macintyre & Co Limited had become strained – even acrimonious. It was the name 'Moorcroft' which had become famous in the world of the applied arts, and not that of James Macintyre & Co. The predictable split occurred in 1912, and William Moorcroft led his workforce from Burslem, across Cobridge Park and into a new Moorcroft factory in Sandbach Road substantially funded with Liberty money.

Sadly, everything ground to a halt on the outbreak of the First World War. Almost alone, William Moorcroft kept his new factory running, making white shaving mugs for the troops in the trenches of Flanders and the Somme. Remnants of coloured pieces still on the factory shelves at the outbreak of war, were packed away into the factory cellars in tea chests (there they lay, covered in soot until they were re-discovered by Hugh Edwards - now Moorcroft chairman - and his then partner, Richard Dennis and their respective wives, Maureen and Sally).

The end of the Great War saw a surge of new design work, backed by a growing friendship with Queen Alexandra, and constant support from Liberty & Co. The Pomegranate design was re-launched in soft new colours set against a cobalt blue background: the design was to continue until its demise shortly before the second world war.

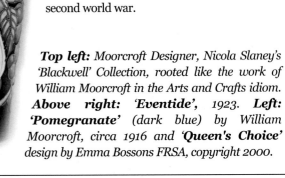

Top left: Moorcroft Designer, Nicola Slaney's 'Blackwell' Collection, rooted like the work of William Moorcroft in the Arts and Crafts idiom. *Above right:* 'Eventide', 1923. *Left:* 'Pomegranate' (dark blue) by William Moorcroft, circa 1916 and 'Queen's Choice' design by Emma Bossons FRSA, copyright 2000.

Ropers sold their controlling shareholding to Hugh and Maureen Edwards, long-standing Moorcroft collectors, and to Richard and Sally Dennis a publisher/antique dealer and a designer respectively.

Although the depth and stature of design under the stewardship of Walter Moorcroft declined markedly, his Magnolia, Hibiscus, Anemone and Clematis pieces served the company well. Even so, and almost inevitably, the limited nature of the design subject matter first caused stress within the company and then outright financial hardship. Today, Moorcroft operates out of what it calls its fifteen Design Windows. Five of these had originally been opened by William himself, but even before 1980, only one Design Window remained open. 'Broad Florals' were all that Moorcroft had to offer. The glorious variety that the William Moorcroft era introduced, had evaporated into thin air.

On the 16 September, 1986, the new owners swept through the old Moorcroft Works, bringing with them fresh ideas. The ancient tea chests which had lain in the cellar since 1914 were unpacked, and the soot-covered contents cleaned and polished. From those pieces, the foundations of a new Moorcroft Museum were laid.

'Pomegranate' was later joined by two of William's most famous landscape designs, Moonlit Blue (1922), and Eventide (1923). Fame followed the popularity of the new work and in 1928, W Moorcroft Limited, was appointed Potters to Her Majesty the Queen, an honour of which William himself was justifiably proud.

William had been joined by his son, Walter, in the mid 1930s. In 1939, Walter joined the army in military intelligence, where he served throughout the Second World War. He was demobbed in 1945, shortly after his father suffered a severe stroke.

Almost immediately, on the 15 October, 1945, William Moorcroft died. Walter took on the company at the point where his father had left off. Flambé work, started by William in 1919, reached new heights of excellence under Walter and only ended with the arrival of a Clean Air Act in 1970. Carbon monoxide was a toxic bi-product which belched out into the atmosphere during the firing process, while the fashionable red tones were enhanced with a wicked lead glaze. Today, although Moorcroft knows the secrets of flambé production, it has never sought to re-introduce the subtle, blood-red pieces.

During his working lifetime of 48 years, William Moorcroft produced 64 new designs. Walter Moorcroft introduced 18 new designs in a career which spanned 46 years. The decline in design output precipitated the virtual collapse of Moorcroft in both 1984 and in 1986. In 1984, new owners arrived in the form of the Roper Brothers, owners of Churchill China. Heroically, they acquired Moorcroft to save it from financial oblivion, but by 1986, things had gone from bad to worse, and in that year the

Top left: Walter Moorcroft with 'After The Storm', 1997.
Above right: Artist painting 'Queen's Choice' design by Emma Bossons FRSA. **Below:** *The Moorcroft museum today which includes designs from William and Walter Moorcroft and members of the Moorcroft Design Studio.*

Window with Reeds at Sunset (Richardson) and Mamoura (Tuffin). Sally single-handedly opened a new Geometric Design Window for the very first time with her Violet and Rose designs. Jointly with Philip, Sally introduced birds into Moorcroft art. A brand new Birds Design Window saw Finches from Tuffin (an echo back to William Moorcroft's Pomegranate design), and Herons from Richardson. Animals in the form of Polar Bears entered an Animals Design Window, again from the hand of Sally Tuffin. Although Sally left the company in 1992, the Animals and Birds Design Windows produces some of the most popular Moorcroft designs worldwide today.

After Sally Tuffin left in 1992, the void was quickly filled by Rachel Bishop, then an unknown designer just 24 years old. Demand for her new designs came thick and fast, so much so that in 1997, the year of the Moorcroft centenary, a brand new Moorcroft Design Studio was formed with Rachel at its head.

The surviving bottle oven was lovingly restored, and the old factory shop, with its dangling white-washed wires and pipes, was renovated to form the Moorcroft Heritage Visitor Centre which itself houses the Moorcroft Museum and the surviving bottle oven. Visitors can climb inside and look at the place in which the first pieces of Moorcroft pottery to emerge from the Sandbach Road factory were fired.

Between 1986 and 1992 design underwent a metamorphosis at the hands of Sally Tuffin and the art master at her former school, Philip Richardson. Sally and Philip between them re-opened the Landscape Design

Under her stewardship, William's Structured and Florian Design Window was re-opened with famous pieces including Solomon (2004) and Tudric Dream (2005).

Thankfully, all pressures to increase the size of the company have fallen on deaf ears. The old art pottery is still just as it has always been, personal, friendly and

Top left: *Senior Designer, Rachel Bishop, in the Moorcroft Design Studio.* **Left:** *'Finches Green and Blue' by Sally Tuffin.* **Above:** *'Tudric Dream' by Rachel Bishop, 2005.*

small. And all of its pottery is still entirely made by hand in Stoke-on-Trent. Today, Moorcroft is as busy as it has ever been, even in its heyday in the 1920s. Designs flow thick and fast from the four current members of the Design Studio, Emma Bossons FRSA, Kerry Goodwin and Nicola Slaney, still led by Rachel Bishop.

The Moorcroft factory is open to all who would like to book a factory tour. Visitors can see Moorcroft pottery being made in just the same way as it was well over a century ago. The Moorcroft Museum and its cellar treasures is a feast for the eye, while the Heritage Visitor Centre has on show pieces of Moorcroft still made in the factory today. Small wonder that Moorcroft pottery, both old and not-so-old, fetches huge prices in the major salerooms of the world.

Left: 'Cloud Nine' by Emma Bossons FRSA uses the industrial imagery of the past but interestingly, weaves flowers into bottle ovens. The creative symbol of pottery, huge belching bottle ovens, have now become art themselves.
Bottom inset: *Emma Bossons pictured inside a bottle oven.*
Bottom: *The Moorcroft Heritage Visitor Centre , 2010.*

To find out more about the Moorcroft story go to www.moorcroft.com or email: enquiries@moorcroft.com. For enquiries about the museum opening times, factory shop and Heritage Visitors Centre tours telephone: 01782 820515.

Garners Garden Centre - A Growing Reputation

What did people used to do at weekends before garden centres were invented? Older readers will recall the days when all shops were closed on Sunday, pubs opened but briefly at lunchtime, and the only 'recreational activities available were a trip to church or Sunday school dressed in one's Sunday best clothes followed by a walk to take tea with a grandparent or aged aunt.

Today, the pubs are open all day. The idea of 'Sunday best' clothes

sounds as archaic as top hats and spats, and many shops open seven days a week. And undoubtedly one of the greatest beneficiary of our more relaxed and liberal modern day attitude to the seventh day of the week have been garden centres.

With over a century and a half of experience behind it, Garners Garden Centre, located on Cemetery Road, Silverdale, is still a family run

Above left and left: *A seed list from 1927 and the first shop on Iron Market all decorated for the Prince of Wales' visit in 1924.* ***Above:*** *Annie Garner who took over the running of the shop with her husband Edgar in the 1930s.* ***Below:*** *John 'Jack' Garner, son of Annie and Edgar, who started a farm seed business at the back of the Iron Market shop.*

business with friendly staff who provide expert advice to everyone who calls in there.

In addition to gardening products and services there are also pet, craft and gift departments. The centre also stocks a large range of garden furniture, tools and DIY equipment in addition to a wide selection of discount Regatta clothing, footwear, rucksacks and travel accessories.

Visitors can now even make the most of their visit by relaxing in a newly-refurbished Barn Restaurant. Have a coffee or tea with a selection of fresh cream cakes, or choose from a menu of freshly-prepared, homemade hot meals.

economic crash after 1929 meant few folk had much money for luxuries. Even so, many still had just sufficient left to buy seeds and bulbs for flowers in their gardens, flowers whose beauty might take their minds from the worry of earning a living – and of the looming threat of German re-armament. Still others recognised

Above: Members of the Garner family pictured outside the Iron Market shop in the early years. *Left:* Annie (right) and staff pictured in 1959. **Below:** Margaret (daughter of Jack Garner)and George Barlow.

The local family business has its origins in Newcastle-under-Lyme where it began life as a seed merchants and florists in the 19th century.

The business was founded by Moses Jenkinson, an ancestor of Edgar Garner after whom today's business took its name.

Even in the 1920s 'Jenkinson's' at 21 Iron Market had been established for so long that it was able to proclaim in its advertising material that the business already had 'over 100 years of practical seed experience attached to it, selecting, improving and raising new and choice seeds of meritorious value for the farm and garden'.

Edgar Garner took over the running of the business in the 1930s and opened a new shop on Iron Market with his wife Annie. The 1930s were a time of hardship for everyone. The

Jack Garner died in 1980 and as a consequence George and Margaret Barlow took over running both sides of the business.

George and Margaret's son David joined the firm that same year, working first in the shop and then selling farm seed. With David's help the business would later enjoy considerable change and expansion.

The plan was to open an out-of-town garden centre. Similar enterprises had begun springing up

that one way to survive in such harsh times was to grow their own vegetables – and to do that one needed vegetable seed.

It was by meeting such demand that Garners, unlike so many businesses, survived the great depression to emerge at the far side of the Second World War able to expand and diversify when economic conditions changed for the better.

Edgar and Annie's son John 'Jack' Garner had taken over the nursery side of the business when his father died.

It was Jack Garner who started a farm seed business at the back of the Iron Market shop in Newcastle, a building known as Steps House, next door to the library.

From Steps House the shop moved to Merrial Street in 1961 and to a warehouse in Pool Dam.

George Barlow married Margaret, Jack Garner's daughter, who worked in Merrial Street. George had joined Garners in 1960 working with Annie.

Annie died in 1969 and George Barlow then took over running the shop, with Jack Garner running the now very successful farm seed supplies business.

all over Britain as increasing prosperity in the 1960s and 1970s had seen more and more people becoming car owners for the first time and able to travel considerable distances to shop.

Having a vision of the future was one thing. Finding a suitable site on which to make that vision a reality was quite another.

At last, seven years after Jack Garner's death, the opportunity to buy land at Silverdale on which to build a garden centre finally presented itself.

Top left: *Garners old shop in Merrial Street in 1991.* **Above:** *The old seed warehouse at Pool Dam.* **Left:** *Garners moved to their new warehouse, pictured left, in 1998.*

Work on the new garden centre began in June, 1987, the year after the Garden Festival. The main shop was to be the greenhouse which had been the entrance of the garden festival in Etruria, Hanley.

Re-erecting the greenhouse in Silverdale was a very experienced builder, Harry Cuthbert, who oversaw the project. Thus the famous Garners Garden Centre was born. David came from the shop to run the new enterprise.

George continued working in the office at the shop in Merrial Street until it closed in 1991. Though the associated pet shop remained in Merrial Street other staff from the garden shop, namely Mark and Keiron, still work in the family business with over 50 years' combined service.

When the Merrial Street shop closed the office was moved to the warehouse at Pool Dam. The warehouse was later sold for the expansion of the BMW garage next door.

Garners farm seed warehouse then moved in across the road from the garden centre and built a new warehouse on Maries Way, off Cemetery Road.

The farm seed side of the business eventually closed when Arthur retired in 2000. The warehouse had been part occupied by a DC Cook car body repair shop, this in turn closed when Business Post occupied the site. It is now home to two new businesses which are thriving there.

Meanwhile, in the years since closing its farm seed business, the Garners Garden Centre has grown and grown, beginning with more under cover facilities, a café and a craft centre.

Today, folk flock to Garners not just on Sundays but every day of the week. The Garden Centre reputation is known not just locally but across the whole region.

This is a business whose reputation is quite literally growing every day.

Top left: David Garner Barlow at work. **Top right:** *David (centre) with the next generation, sons Thomas (left) and William.* **Centre:** *Seed lists from 1953 (centre), 1983 (left) and a 2010 advertising leaflet.* **Below:** *Garners Garden Centre, 2010.*

J & R Hill Ltd - Established 1960

Staffordshire's Leading Supplier of Fireplaces

Based in Whittle Road, Meir Park, Stoke-on-Trent, J & R Hill have one of Staffordshire's most exclusive fireplace factory showrooms. Marble, Stone, Wood and Granite fireplaces feature in this beautiful showroom. Also a range of Multi Fuel/Wood-Burning Stoves and a selection of fireside accessories to add those finishing touches. The sheet metal factory, producing fireplace components sold all over the UK, is impressive, but in 1960 it was so different!

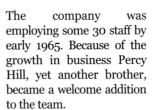

Founder of the business was Joe Hill. Trade was in Joe's blood; his father Richard Hill in the 1920's, was a market trader and had a Fruit and Veg shop in Huntbach Street, Hanley, opposite Sir Stanley Matthew's father's barbershop.

In July, 1960, at the age of 23, Joe, a trained steel fabricator, started his own business in premises in Foley Street, Fenton; they cost him the princely sum of 10 shillings (50p) a week to rent.

Joe's older brother, Reg Hill, a blacksmith by trade, soon joined Joe in business and the firm of J & R Hill Ltd came into being, producing wrought iron gates and small steel fabrications of all kinds.

A year after the business began J & R Hill rented the top floor of a pottery company's premises in Edensor Road, Longton.

Another brother, Fred Hill, now joined the firm. Fred's trade was making fireplaces. His knowledge of the fireplace industry, along with the skill's possessed by Joe and Reg, enabled the company to begin manufacturing stainless steel, brass and copper fire frames, which were soon being sold all over the UK.

By 1964 J & R Hill needed more manufacturing space. Instead of renting extra space the company bought the whole building in Edensor Road. At the same time a new entrance was constructed from Barford Street which became the firm's new address.

The company was employing some 30 staff by early 1965. Because of the growth in business Percy Hill, yet another brother, became a welcome addition to the team.

Top left: *Father, Richard Hill, in the 1920s outside his shop in Huntbach Street, Hanley, who was the inspiration for Joe Hill to set up his own business.* *Below left:* *Aerial view and circled view of Barford Street Factory in 1964.* *Below:* *Original premises in Foley Street, Fenton.* *Above:* *An early brochure advertising the company's adjustable gates.*

In 1969 the company appointed Timber & Tile Ltd, a company based in Newry, Northern Ireland, as its agent. Timber & Tile would distribute all the fireplace products in Northern Ireland and in Eire. The companies have traded together for over 40 years, and the working relationship is as strong now as back in 1969.

Meanwhile Reg Hill left the company and his brother Percy took over the office and administration side of the business.

Fireplace surrounds, however, were not the company's only products.

In 1972 Joe Hill had the idea of producing stainless steel exhausts for cars.

Hill's Stainless Steel Exhausts Ltd was formed in 1973. Manufacture and production was the responsibility of Fred Hill. Fred produced an exhaust for the Mini car costing only 50p more than a standard exhaust but with a lifetime guarantee – or at least as long as the purchaser owned the car.

Sadly, Hill's Stainless Steel Exhausts ceased trading in 1975. Apparently the car industry didn't want a product which came with a lifetime guarantee!

In 1974 Rob Hill, Joe's son, joined the company from school at the age of 16 years.

During Edward Heath's Conservative Government in the early 1970s the three-day week caused all sorts of manufacturing problems. Despite those problems however the company still grew its steel fabrications and fireplace business.

So significant was growth that 1976 saw a large increase in orders, which led to additional storage being rented in Fenton and Weston Coyney. The company now employed 40 staff, and most importantly had received orders from British Coal for refurbishing bunker and coalface equipment.

In February, 1978, building contractors moved on to a two-acre site for a new factory on the Meir Park Industrial Estate. In July of that year, the fabrication section of J&R Hill Ltd came into being. The covered floor space was 10,000 sq. ft. Within 12 months of moving into the new factory however circumstances dictated that the working area needed to be doubled to cope with the increasing volume of activity. In May 1980 work commenced on an extension to the new factory, giving a total covered floor space of 20,000 sq. ft.

*Top: J & R Hill's Whittle Road premises. **Above left:** The Hill brothers, L-R: Joe, Percy and Fred. **Below left:** The old logo for Hill's Stainless Steel Exhausts Ltd. **Below:** Steel fabrication.*

Following the move of the company's fabrication section from the Barford Street factory, the fireplace component section found it had a great deal more space: it was now able to expand to such a degree that it became one of the largest manufacturers of fireplace components in the UK.

Fred and Percy Hill ran the fireplace side of the business and would exhibit the firm's products locally at the Kings Hall, Stoke.

Meanwhile, John Large, who had worked for the company since 1965, became a Director of J & R Hill in 1979. John's ability, drive and knowledge of steel fabrication made him a key member of the management team. Joe Hill and John Large pushed the steel fabrication side of the business and now obtained national contracts with British Coal.
By 1984 the company had 80 staff. Yet difficult times lay ahead.

That year the miners' strike affected the whole of the country and in particular J & R Hill. Six years later British Coal would be closed, and overnight J & R Hill would lose 60% of its sales.

In 1988 John Hill, Joe's son now joined the family firm. British Coal refurbishment work was still on going alongside general steel fabrication for Edwards & Jones and other local companies.

In the early 1990s, at a cost of £100,000, again the company extended their Whittle Road premises for refuse vehicle refurbishment. J & R Hill moved into refurbishing refuse collection vehicles for councils all over the country. Orders came from Chesterfield, Braintree, Crewe and Nantwich, Harringay and Stoke-on-Trent as well as from private companies such as Biffa Waste, Cory Environmental, Service Team and Arthur Wrights.

In 1994, the Directors decided to close the Barford Street, Longton factory and built a 13,000 sq. ft unit at their Whittle Road site. A showroom was also built, adjoining the new unit. The total cost was some £250,000. Robert Hill's daughter Lisa joined the business in 1996 followed two years later by her brother, Adam.

J & R Hill Ltd now moved into Automatic Barrier Systems designed and manufactured by the company itself. The

Top left and above:
December 1988: "Lorry Pull" from Lautreks Car Park, Weston Coyney area to Signal Radio in Shelton, Stoke. The Pull was for the Denise Morse Charity. Denise was a local lady who was terminally ill and raised money for the Bone Marrow charity before she died. She even made it to the Terry Wogan Show. J & R Hill raised over £5,500.

Above left: *Brochures from the company's Refuse and Automatic Barrier Systems businesses.*

In 2006, Robert Hill designed a collection of pure marble, micro marble and stone fireplaces which are now being manufactured in the company's factory in China. There are 25 staff employed there. The finest Spanish marble is shipped from Spain to China. The fireplaces are sold under the name of Luxus, a trade name owned by J & R Hill. The fireplaces are shipped from China to the company's premises in Meir Park, where they are checked and dispatched to customers all over the British Isles.

The company celebrated its 50th birthday in July, 2010. After half a century in business much has changed. Percy Hill retired in 1984, Fred Hill in 1992 and Joe Hill in 2002. Today, not even the company's longest serving member of staff, Mr. J Dyke, with 44 years under his belt and still going strong, was there at the very beginning.

system was called The Hill Stop and was used for vehicle control and security. The firm also designed and began manufacturing Telescopic Manual Bollard Security posts.

The company began making Sovereign Gas Fires in 1996. Owned by J & R Hill, these gas fires were sold to gas fire showrooms across the country, and through the firm's own showroom at Whittle Road.

The showroom was extended in 1999 at a cost of £50,000.

But if fires and fireplaces were a growing part of the business, steel fabrication was declining. In 2000 the firm closed its steel fabrication department due to British Coal pit closures, Edwards & Jones Ltd had been sold and the demise of local engineering. The fabrication unit is still owned by J & R Hill and is leased to another local business.

J & R Hill Ltd now focused increasingly on its fireplace showroom and sales, though still manufacturing a wide range of products for the fireplace industry, including brass and stainless steel frames, hearth plates, bespoke inglenook canopies and reinforcing.

Yet, as a new generation takes the firm forward in the 21st century one thing is constant: a commitment to ensuring that J & R Hill Ltd remains a family firm dedicated to always meeting its customers' expectations of the very best.

Top left: A J&R Hill exhibition stand in Harrogate in June 1998. **Below and bottom:** Interior and exterior shots of the J&R Hill Whittle Road showroom.

James T Blakeman & Co. - A Sizzling Success

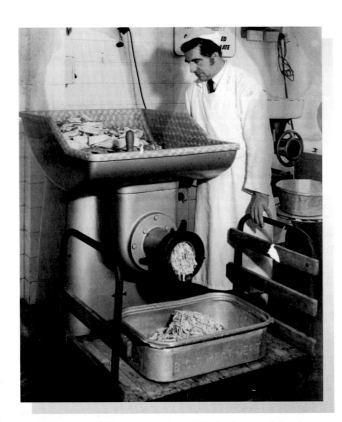

James T Blakeman & Co Ltd is the home of the famous Supreme Sausage. Now one of Europe's leading manufacturers of sausage and meat products, the Blakeman family business has been supplying the domestic, export, catering and fast food markets for over half a century.

After the Second World War, during which he had served in the RAF, James Blakeman spent a short time as manufacturing supervisor with a pork butcher in Leek, Staffordshire.

In 1953, having picked up what he needed to know about the business, Jim decided to set up on his own. He started small, taking a mobile refreshment bar in partnership with his brother-in-law, and at the same time worked as a freelance sausage-meat manufacturer.

After his marriage to Ann in 1955 the couple bought a farm at Caverswall, near Stoke-on-Trent, turning cow sheds and stables at the back into a small manufacturing unit for sausage, cooked meats and poultry. It was a modest enterprise, turning out 300 lbs. of sausage per week on small, hand-operated machines. Soon though, Jim, and Ann (who would be a mainstay of the business until her retirement in 1995), moved up into larger quantity production with an 'Alexander Werk' filler and a 'Seydlemann' bowl chopper. The weekly sausage production at the farm soon topped the three-ton mark.

The Blakeman's son, Philip, the current Managing Director would complete an apprenticeship that included learning every process in the small factory, and later gained an HGV1 licence to drive the company's refrigerated delivery trucks. Eighty-hour weeks were the norm rather than the exception as he followed the same work ethic as his parents.

In 1977 Blakeman's moved to larger, modern factory premises at Northam Road, Hanley. Included in the £250,000 investment were new mincers, fillers, massagers and a 80-litre Alpina Bowl Cutter. Production steadily rose to seven tonnes of sausage per week.

The product range covered Supreme Quality Sausages and a

Top left: Founder James T. Blakeman working on one of the first production machines on the farm in 1960. Above: First market stall in Hanley in 1954. Left: An early delivery bike.

Catering Sausage. There was even a deep-fry version for distribution to chip shops, canteens and motorway restaurants. In addition the company prepared a range of cooked meats. The firm covered a 100 mile radius from Stoke, though during the summer season, products were soon being taken by customers as far away as Cornwall.

In 1988 Blakeman's moved to showpiece premises in Trubshaw Cross, Longport. At this £650,000 self-contained factory Blakeman's had a clinically hygienic open plan working area of 40,000 sq.ft.

The Blakemans' daughter, Susan, now Finance Director, completed the family team when she joined the firm in 1982 to work in administration and accounts, later adding training to her responsibilities.

The firm's EEC appointment, setting the highest standards possible for quality and hygiene within the food industry, was complemented by its membership of the British Frozen Food Federation, the Institute of Meat and the in-house training in Advanced Food Hygiene. Quality and Hygiene are as much a part of the ingredients of a Blakeman's Sausage as the prime products and the secret seasoning they contain.

Ever since James Blakeman hit on the right mix of seasoning to produce that special something that gave his sausages their special taste, the secret formula has been kept under lock and key.

Now one of the UK's leading manufacturers of sausage and meat products, J T Blakeman and Co has opened a new industry-leading production facility that houses all of its operations under one roof.

The new £4m facility in Millennium Way, High Carr Business Park, Newcastle-under-Lyme, will allow Blakeman's to accommodate ever-increasing orders from its customers. Managing Director, Philip Blakeman, explains: "We've been committed to supplying the catering and fast food industries with the highest quality product for over 50 years and we've demonstrated our commitment to the future of the industry by making this investment. Production capacity has doubled."

Above left: The Mayor pays a visit to Blakemans. Above right: A view inside Blakemans in 1980. Below: The new £4m extension to the original plant at Millennium Way, High Carr Business Park, Newcastle-under-Lyme.

A focus on quality has made Blakeman's a leading supplier to both UK and foreign markets with a worldwide distribution of 12,000 tonnes of its products a year, and an annual turnover of £22m.

Since the 1950s the Blakeman family has kept pace with the changing demands of its customers by developing a range of over 50 unbeatable products, ranging from the standard catering pork and the exotic pork, red pepper and coriander recipe, to a Cumberland pork pattie and Moroccan style lamb meatballs.

Blakeman's specialist cooking and cold storage operation was formed in 2000 shortly after Philip Blakeman and his sister, Financial Director Susan Cope, took over running the business from their father Jim, now Chairman.

According to Jim Blakeman "Since Philip and Susan took over they've consolidated our position in the frozen and chilled markets and moved us successfully into new cooked markets by following the core principles we've always employed."

In an expanding market that requires the convenience of a ready cooked products, Blakeman's has the facilities to provide deep fry, oven and steamed products. Indeed its cooking plant, which services the ready meal and contract cooking markets, has the capacity to produce 100,000 standard size sausages every eight hours. The new facility also includes a cold store, warehouse, offices and staff facilities.

Bespoke recipes can be formulated in the development kitchen where Blakeman's professional development chefs work with the clients who can now be involved in the process of developing products.

"Our development kitchen offers clients the opportunity to develop products to their own specification and fine tune them for taste, texture and appearance," explains Philip.

To achieve consistently high standards only pork from EU-approved suppliers is used, along with ingredients from a range of long-standing suppliers with proven quality standards. "These cuts are more expensive, which can be a challenge, but we are committed to maintaining the quality that we are known for," says Philip.

A second key principle has been investing in the most efficient manufacturing processes, whether plant, machinery, recruitment, training or quality assurance systems. Philip Blakeman says: "The majority of our 120 employees are long-standing and we send our management teams on external courses. We also employ consultants who regularly advise and work with us on ever-changing legislation. Our in-house training is always up to date."

By combining ingredients of the highest quality, and fully-qualified staff with the world's best equipment Blakeman's

*Top: Blakemans nostalgic advertising. **Left:** A view inside Blakemans state-of-the-art facility. **Above:** The Blakeman range.*

£8.5m facility is a showpiece for the hygienic handling of food conforming to all current European legislation.

The new industry-leading design of the factory is one of the most advanced in Europe, with the lowest carbon footprint for a development of its type. According to Philip: "The building uses energy efficient lighting throughout with lighting sensors and we have replaced our gas fridges with eco-friendly ones. We also recycle all of our waste and our package is locally sourced, which reduces vehicle miles."

Blakeman's has had a fully integrated IT system that links every departmental function since 'efsis' issued guidelines on 'instant time live data' standards in 2005. The system known as Tropos, supplied by SSI, provides real-time, full traceability of ingredients throughout the production process, all carried out through touch screen technology. "We've always invested in the latest plant and equipment and our IT systems are of an equivalent standard to improve efficiency and reduce costs. This has been fundamental in us attracting a number of new clients, all of whom continue to benefit from the investment we have continually made in state-of-the-art manufacturing, storage and distribution systems, which has resulted in an operation that is widely regarded as a model to the rest of Europe," says Philip.

Blakeman's also operates a fleet of state-of-the-art temperature-controlled vehicles that deliver products raw, cooked, frozen and chilled throughout Great Britain. European deliveries are made by specialist continental temperature-controlled logistics companies. Operating 24 hours a day, the new facility provides overnight parking, showers and catering facilities for regular drivers.

Despite having the capacity to double its already impressive output, Philip Blakeman wants to grow the business at a steady controlled rate, as this type of growth means it can maintain the quality systems and products, which have become synonymous with Blakeman's. "Carefully staged growth will benefit our customers - as a company we've achieved our market position by focusing on doing the basics consistently well. That focus positioned us strongly to proceed with our new facility. We have put ourselves where we can maintain our position in the market, and maintain the Blakeman brand in the market for many years to come, to the long term benefit of our customers and staff," he said.

*Top: Part of the Blakemans fleet. **Left:** Blakemans delicious meatballs. **Below:** Chairman and founder James T. Blakeman with his late wife Ann, his son Philip Blakeman and daughter Susan Cope.*

Rafferty Steeplejacks - Climbing For Industry

Rafferty Steeplejacks located at Nash Peake Works, Tunstall, are the UK's leading industrial chimney specialist. Since the 1940s the firm has been responsible for transforming the skyline of the Potteries.

Rafferty Steeplejacks was formed as a result of Sam Rafferty being a paratrooper with the 6th Airborne Division during World War II.

Born in 1923, Sam came from a very poor working class family. He worked down the Chatterley Whitfield coal mine as a pan lad from the age of just eleven. Once he was buried alive for two days until he was rescued. He continued to work down the pit until he was 14 years old.

Jumping out of aeroplanes into battle was a new concept in the Second World War. That novelty and Sam's natural sense of adventure led to him joining the 8th parachute battalion, 3rd parachute brigade of the 6th Airborne Division, right from its formation. Sam parachuted into Normandy in France on D Day, 6 June, 1944. He survived that harrowing experience only to be sent to the Ardennes in late 1944.

On his return to England, Sam, by then a combat veteran, started to prepare for what would be his final parachute jump over the Rhine into Germany. On 24 March, 1945, Operation Varsity began. Sam and his brave comrades of the 6th Airborne Division were about to embark on an adventure which would eventually climax in the end of the war in Europe.

The photograph at the below left shows Sam with paratroopers of 5 Platoon, B Company just prior to the Airbornes drop over the Rhine into Germany.

By the age of 22 Sam was one of the few paratroopers to survive all three major World War II combat operations involving the 6th Airborne Division. After the war ended he was sent to Palestine, where he was finally demobbed from the Parachute Regiment in 1946.

On his return home to England, Sam initially found it difficult to adjust to civilian life. With work in short supply he was about to rejoin the Parachute Regiment to make a career in the Army: he thought nothing could match the thrill of jumping out of aeroplanes. That was until, on the very day he was to re-enlist in the army, he saw two steeplejacks swinging on bosuns chairs working high up on a 300-foot brick chimney.

Left: *Sam Rafferty is pictured on the front row right, with Paratroopers of 5 Platoon, B Company just prior to the Airborne drop over the Rhine into Germany.* ***Top:*** *Sam Rafferty at work in the late 1940s.*

pottery industry. The Rafferty Brothers became minor celebrities amongst the people of Stoke-on-Trent they were unique, five brothers from the same family doing what was, and still is, regarded as one of the most hazardous jobs in modern industry.

Over the decades Sam and his four younger brothers demolished the majority of the brick chimneys in the area and, more than any other firm, were responsible for cleaning up smokey old Stoke.

Chimney inspection and maintenance are a core business of Rafferty Chimneys, with inspection and maintenance service covering all types of chimney structures.

Raffertys inspection and maintenance service first applies sophisticated technical skills and visual evidencing techniques to assess the condition of any chimney whether brick, steel or concrete chimneys, irrespective of processing function.

As part of its service, Rafferty Chimneys also supplies crucial servicing to lightning protection systems fitted to all types of industrial chimneys. As part of routine chimney inspections, all lightning conductor sytems that are fitted to chimneys are inspected and tested for earth resistance and continuity to ensure that they meet the requirements of the relevant standards.

With little or no health and safety regulations in those days, the steeplejacks allowed Sam to climb up and join them. He was immediately hooked by the danger and thrill of the job. He claimed that in Civvy Street this job was the very next best thing to being a paratrooper. And so with his head for heights and nerves of steel Sam became a steeplejack himself.

It was not only good nerves and a head for height which Sam had gained as a paratrooper: his military service had also given him self-belief and self-confidence.

That belief and confidence made Sam determined to make something of himself. He initially learned the trade working for other steeplejack firms. In 1949, however, Sam set up his own business in Tunstall and employed his four younger brothers Harry, Joe, Kenny and Ron and the thriving business became a limited company on 12 April, 1954.

In those days the Potteries, was a steeplejacks paradise, with hundreds of brick chimneys and bottle neck ovens servicing the

In addition, Raffertys also remains one of the country's leading companies able to address and overcome the difficulties involved in major demolition and dismantling contracts, particularly within sensitive, densely-populated and live situations.

Inspection, maintenance and demolition is only part of the story. The company manufactures not only chimneys but also a wide variety of related products.

Top left and above right: *The Rafferty brothers at work in the early days.* ***Left:*** *Sam Rafferty briefing the crew, early 1950s.*

The company now has the facilities to produce all types of high quality fabrications to customer requirements. These include workshop housing of 15,000 Sq ft, four, 5-ton overhead cranes, heavy duty rolls, guillotines and welding machinery. All of which complement the highly-skilled workforce and help to achieve quality fabrications in both ferrous and nonferrous materials.

Though chimney design and manufacture remains the core business the company designs and supplies a wide range of fabrications such as Access Platforms, Fire Escapes, Walkways, Tanks, Support Steelwork, Afterburner Exhausts and Kiln Fabrications.

The complexity of chimney design and manufacture today involves both technology and science. The ever-increasing stringency of environmental considerations and legislation has led to ever more demanding performance criteria.

Computer aided design is used for the development of all chimney types including: self supporting, guy supported, single flue, multiflue, insulated and clad, twin skin, refractory lined, lattice tower and flues, new flues to existing chimneys and to determine chimney height requirements.

Each new installation must now comply with not only basic standards of operational safety and efficiency, but also conform to current and projected regulations for factory pollution, clean air acts and the control of energy consumption.

There are many more crucial areas of specification than existed when the company began trading. Raffertys has evolved to always maintain a vanguard position ahead of both statutory requirements and its competitors.

Installations are carried out by skilled, trained and specialised staff. From Tunstall the precise and safe installation of Raffertys new steel chimneys have been carried out all over the world.

In the Caribbean a 60m high reinforced concrete chimney was refurbished at a sugar refinery on the island St Kitts, whilst in Trinidad and Tobago the company was contracted to inspect and make major repairs to a 70m high steel chimney at a power station. Also in the Dominican Republic a major refurbishment was made to a 50m high reinforced concrete chimney on a sugar refinery, as well as the demolition of a 65m high brick chimney on a sugar refinery. In the Middle-East Raffertys went to Kuwait to inspect a 180m high reinforced concrete chimney at a power station. The dismantling of a 60m high steel chimney was another international contract at an oil refinery in Kenya.

In colder climes the company went to Iceland to refurbish of a 75m high reinforced concrete chimney at a cement works and in Lithuania

Top left: Three of the many accreditations awarded to the company. Left: A fabulous picture that shows the awesome heights Raffertys steeplejacks have to scale to inspect and repair chimneys. Above: On site erection.

major refurbishment of a 123m high reinforced concrete chimney at an oil refinery was undertaken by the firm.

Since its formation, Raffertys has continued to invest in growth and diversification, with uncompromising standards to their inspection and maintenance services, to building its engineering base to research and develop market leading technologies.

Left: Inspection and repair works to 123.18m High Reinforced Concrete Chimney at AB Mazeikiu Nafta Oil Refinery, Lithuania, 2005/2006. Above: One of Raffertys young trainee steeplejacks namely Dominic Powner, winning a top award at the C.I.T.B. run Bircham Newton training school for steeplejacks. Raffertys endeavour to invest time and expense into bringing young people into the industry and their commitment to training both on and off site was highlighted in this award. Below: Matt Rafferty following in his father's and grandfather's footsteps as the third generation of Rafferty steeplejacks. Bottom: Rafferty Chimneys, Nash Peake Works, Tunstall.

Today, with decades of experience behind it, Raffertys operates throughout the U.K, Europe and the world. It is the UKs leading specialist in all aspects of industrial chimney engineering, from inspection, maintenance and demolition, to the design, manufacture and erection of new steel chimneys.

Sam worked hard all his life. The company he established is now run by his only son Nick. The third generation of Raffertys, Sams two grandsons Matthew and Daniel also work for the company. Sam, who died in 1993, lived to see his company grow from humble beginnings to national and international status. His proud son and grandsons are determined to continue with the traditions he so strongly believed in and trusted.

Keeling & Walker - From Stoke to the World

As the world's largest producer of tin oxides, Keeling & Walker Ltd, based in Whieldon Road, Stoke-on-Trent, is a name to be reckoned with. Company founder Frank Keeling was born in 1880 in Newcastle-under-Lyme, Staffordshire, and educated at the High School. In 1902 he married May, the daughter of Abraham Fielding. Mr Fielding helped Frank during his early years, when he was beginning to build up a business as a potters' merchant. By 1914 the business had expanded sufficiently for new and larger buildings to be constructed at the present site consisting of offices, stores and workshops for the preparation of glazes, frits and colours.

The firm had been named Keeling & Walker (Walker being the maiden name of Frank's mother) but it was not until 1916 that it became a Limited company. By then it was a leading supplier of all types of potters' materials, consumables, plant and equipment, and was the authorised agent for Cookson's white lead and Pike's ball clay.

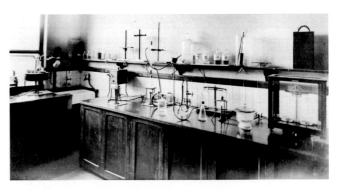

The potters' merchant business continued in the twenties, together with the ball clay agency. During the 1914-18 war the Company made millions of dust respirators for munitions factories. Preferred for their lightness and simplicity, similar models continued in manufacture until the 1980s. Aluminium mould natches, valued for their accurate registration properties, were manufactured from the early days until 2008. They were supplied to many manufacturers of the plaster of paris moulds used to make holloware and sanitaryware.

Left: *A very early brochure displaying Keeling & Walker's wares.* **Above:** *A view inside an early laboratory.* **Below:** *Keeling & Walker's Whieldon Road premises in 1914.*

Since the 1990s the Company has continued to specialise in tin oxide based materials. A key factor in continuing growth has been producing innovative materials tailored to customers' specific requirements.

In 1998 the Company acquired the tin oxide manufacturing business of its main European rival T.H. Goldschmidt Ag. The addition of the 'Thermox' range of materials transformed the business from being a major international supplier of tin oxide into the World Leader.

Frank Keeling realised the growing importance of tin oxide, which was used for ceramic pigments and as an opacifier in ceramic glazes and vitreous enamels. By 1932 he had developed an improved method of tin oxide production - the precursor of the present 'Superlite' thermal process. By 1939 tin oxide was the main product.

In 1945 Frank Keeling, by then aged 65, was joined by his son-in-law, Guy German. He concentrated on founding an export market. With the help of Norman Sinclair, who had originally made his reputation as a colour chemist and manufacturer, special grades were developed, and by 1955 Keeling & Walker was exporting 40% of its production. Guy German remained on the Board as Chairman until 1978.

In 1964 a controlling interest in the Company was acquired by the Patino Group, represented then by Consolidated Tin Smelters, whose successor, Amalgamated Metal Corporation Plc, is still the parent company.

Frank Keeling died in 1958, and in 1959 his grandson David German joined the Company. In 1960 the tin oxide production area was enlarged, and the plant extended and modernised. In 1965 metastannic acid - a hydrated form of tin oxide - was added to the product range, and a year later atomised tin powder. David German retired as Managing Director in 1991, following the acquisition by Amalgamated Metal Corporation of the remaining privately-owned shares.

The rate of new product development accelerated from the 1970s. In 1985 the Company was a pioneer in the development of ATO (antimony tin oxide) nanomaterials. The combination of optical transparency and electrical conductivity that these materials offer resulted in continuing demand for over three decades.

Alistair Borthwick took over from David German as Managing Director in 1991. Upon his death in 2003 Alistair was succeeded by Stephen Lipiec (previously the Technical Director). Current key personnel include Michael Wood (Business Manager and Company Secretary) who, having joined in 1962, is the Company's longest serving employee, and Martyn Pedley (Operations Manager), who joined in 2006.

Today the Company produces many grades of tin oxide, metastannic acid, antimony tin oxide, tin powders and granules, and other specialised materials used in ceramics, the automobile industry, glass manufacture and electrical contact applications, to name but a few.

Some 95% of output is now exported. Keeling & Walker continues to specialise and excel in its core expertise, and to deliver innovative products supported by continuous investment in state-of-the art production facilities.

Top left: *Female staff making dust respirators for the munitions factories during the First World War.* ***Centre and below:*** *The old company kiln logo which can still be seen today on the outside of the Keeling & Walker building, pictured below.*

Walkers Nonsuch - Favourite Toffees for Generations

Walkers' Nonsuch Ltd, based in Calverley Street, Longton, Stoke-on-Trent is one of England's oldest makers of traditional toffee. The family-owned company has been making toffee to its traditional recipes since the turn of the 20th century.

Walkers' remains at the forefront of the toffee market, supplying its world famous toffee to customers in more than 35 countries.

Toffee production is now managed by Ian Walker, grandson of the company founder, Edward Joseph Walker.

The traditional family recipe has changed very little over the past 100 years. Walkers' still uses only the finest natural ingredients in its toffee - whole milk, sugar enhanced with molasses, real chocolate with high minimum cocoa solids and lashings of butter added in the final processes of cooking to ensure a rich and creamy taste.

Former potter, Edward Joseph Walker, opened a small sweet shop in Longton, along with his sister, Florence, who helped out in the shop and managed the books for him.

Edward began to sell a selection of toffee made in the back of the shop to his own recipes. Demand for Edward's homemade toffee grew so rapidly however, that he was forced to open a small factory in the old King Street area of Longton to cope, followed later by premises in Sutherland Road.

In 1915 Edward brought in his son, Edward Victor, to help with production. Together they manufactured their toffee, one batch at a time to Edward's original recipe. The business became an independent company with limited liability in 1922.

Walkers' Nonsuch takes its name from Henry VIII's famous Nonsuch Palace built in 1538. Dubbed the 'palace of all palaces' for its exquisite splendour there was 'nonsuch' like it. This was exactly like the reputation of Edward's delicious toffee, with 'nonsuch' like it either.

Business flourished and Edward Walker's Nonsuch toffee was enjoyed by an ever increasing number of customers. However, from the outbreak of the Second World War, and in the immediate post war years, the firm was forced to restrict its output, finding it increasingly difficult to source its raw materials.

When import restrictions and sweet rationing were eventually lifted business began to grow again and Walkers' decided to move to larger premises. The new site on Calverley Street, Longton, had been a sweet factory ever since it was built in 1894. It had previously belonging to boiled sweet manufacturers, Horleston Brothers Ltd, a firm which Walkers' had

Top left: *Founder, Edward Joseph Walker.* ***Top right:*** *Where it all began, the company's first shop.* ***Left:*** *Two early delivery vehicles.*

acquired in 1947. Another firm, Siddalls Blue Churn Confectionery, was acquired in 1961.

On the death of Edward Victor Walker in 1962 Ian Walker and his brother Edward became joint managing directors of the family firm. The brothers set about investing in modern equipment enabling them to produce Walkers' toffees by the ton. Ian and Edward watched over the production at every stage to ensure that the toffee always met the exacting standards set by their father and grandfather before them.

Firmly established in the Midlands, the popularity of Walkers' toffee soon spread to the whole of the United Kingdom and even further afield. During the 1950s the company began to receive enquiries from export buyers.

Increasing production in the 1970s made it possible for Walkers' to seriously consider supplying overseas markets. Today exports are a key area of business with customers in dozens of different countries enjoying the pure taste of Walkers' Nonsuch toffee.

Edward walker passed away in 1981, however, his brother Ian remains Managing Director.

Whilst Walkers' recipes have changed very little, great advances have been made in technology and packaging. A continual programme of investment in specialist equipment has resulted in an increase in efficiency and speed of production, whilst maintaining the consistency and quality of the finished product.

Down the years staff numbers have risen to fifty. Particularly notable was the late Cyril Jackson, Company Secretary, who was with the business for fifty years. Adrian Hill is Operations Director with over a quarter of a century with the firm. But Walkers' Nonsuch Ltd continues to be a family concern, with Ian at the helm, and daughters, Kate and Emma, Directors involved in sales and marketing. Nephew Edward Nicholas Walker is Director responsible for production.

Meanwhile quality and taste remain second to none – there's still nonsuch like Walkers' toffee.

Top and centre: A selection of Walkers Nonsuch toffees. ***Below left:*** *Walkers hammer pack toffees.* ***Below:*** *The Walker family: Ian (seated) with daughters Emma (centre) and Katie (right) and their cousin Edward (left).*

Clement McGough & Sons - Complete Funeral Directors

Death and taxes are said to be the only certainties in life. In reality some folk do manage to avoid taxes, but there's no avoiding death, it comes to all of us.

The loss of a loved one is always a difficult time for those left behind. Thankfully the profession of funeral director has evolved to help not only organise funerals but also to provide a plethora of sound advice in such difficult days.

One of the longest established and well respected names amongst local Funeral Directors is McGough.

For over seventy years the firm of Clement McGough & Sons has been providing funeral services to folk in Stoke and well beyond.

McGoughs' funeral business was founded in Tunstall by Clement McGough, son of William Peter McGough and Anne Elizabeth Bowles.

Today the firm is still based in Tunstall, at 79 Roundwell Street.

William Peter McGough owned a shop and a haulage business in Nash Peake Street. He was an independent councillor, a Justice of the Peace and a Papal Knight. McGough Street in Tunstall is named after him.

Clement McGough was one of seven children born to William and Ann, two of

whom sadly died young, one as a baby, and a sister at 21 years of age. Clement would eventually marry Ethel Lawrence and together they would have six children of their own, three sons and three daughters: Mararet, Lawrence, Joan, Paul, David (Auxiliary Bishop of Birmingham) and Veronica.

Many long-established firms of funeral directors trace their origins back to joiners who were frequently called upon to manufacture coffins, and who gradually extended their role. McGoughs is no exception.

Initially a brickmaker, Clement later moved to H. & R. Johnson Limited, where he served his apprenticeship in order to become a full-time factory joiner. During the Second World War he was a volunteer in the fire service.

Clement started the funeral business when Fr. Ryan, a local Roman Catholic priest, asked him, while he was helping build the Sacred Heart Church, if Clement would make a coffin for a family who could not afford a funeral. Clement went further. In addition to making the coffin, he dressed up his father's horse and dray and organised the whole event.

Since then McGoughs have offered a continuing caring service to all religious persuasions and all denominations in North Staffordshire and South Cheshire and beyond.

Top: Mr & Mrs Clement McGough. **Left and below:** Two fomer C. McGough & Sons company vehicles.

Unexpected by himself Clement had gone into business as a funeral director, a fact which was announced at the next church service. Initially Clement continued working at H. & R. Johnson, and during this time his father helped in conducting funerals. At that time his future wife Ethel helped in building the business, acting as a secretary and keeping the books. Later when they married, she went into the funeral business full time, still as a secretary and bookkeeper. Clement was one of the first qualified Embalmers in the area in the 1950s.

In addition to conducting funeral services the McGoughs also provided a taxi service, taking many expectant mothers to hospital.

Today the family tradition is carried on by Paul McGough, one of Clement and Ethels's sons, who followed his father into the business. Paul is ably assisted by his wife Brenda, while their eldest son, Tim McGough, is the business manager. There are also two daughters who, in keeping with family tradition, are members of caring professions. Tim McGough and the late Jayne, have two daughters, Georgina and Sophia, and a son named

Callum. Tim is a foundation governor at St. Johns School in Kidsgrove and also a junior rugby coach. Jayne sadly died in 2009.

Over the years additional services have been added to help clients through difficult times. McGoughs can arrange for all practical advice, and help in arranging registration of death and all matters relating to funerals.

A comfortable and spacious lounge is available for clients to meet with their funeral director. There they can arrange for a choice of funeral furniture and accessories. At all times clients wishes are of paramount importance. McGoughs will arrange all press notices and printing, together with floral tributes and catering. They can also provide memorial stones and horse drawn hearses on request if clients so wish. Chapels of rest are available for viewing loved ones in peace and privacy.

McGough's is proud to be the 'Complete Funeral Directors'.

*Top: C. McGough & Sons 79 Roundwell Street, Tunstall, Stoke-on-Trent, premises. **Left:** The team at McGough & Sons, pictured in July, 2010.*

G.C. Dewey & Son Ltd - On The Top Rung

G. C. Dewey & Son Ltd is based at the City Ladder Works, in Victoria Road, Fenton. No prizes for guessing what the firm makes!

The company founder was the eldest of seven, and at his birth in 1903 was the most recent 'George Dewey'. There had been a George Dewey in every generation of his family since 1734.

In 1916, at the age of 13, George started a nine year apprenticeship as a wood turner at Charles Moseley's, of Hanley.

As requirement waned in the 1920s for hand turned products, and the mechanisation of the woodworking industry took hold, Moseley's started to produce ladders. By the 1950s George was now a Director and Manager of Charles Moseley's. When the firm closed it was a natural progression for George to continue under his own name.

The new business commenced at the Old Mill in Shelton in 1953 as wood-turners and ladder-makers.

George had become an acclaimed and renowned wood-turner whose work was revered in books on the subject. He regularly lectured on the subject at Hanley Teacher Training College, which was on the site now occupied by the bus station.

George was soon to be joined full time by his only son Marshall. The company flourished and it soon moved to a new purpose built factory, the 'City Ladder Works' in Victoria Road Fenton. Though Victoria Road has under gone

some changes since 'Dewey's' arrived the company still occupies exactly the same site.

Marshall Dewey, an accomplished wood turner in his own right, was also a talented engineer. Like his father he also lectured at

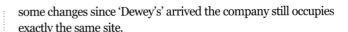
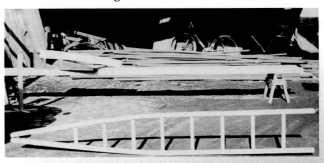

local colleges. Under Marshall's directorship the business diversified. A sideline of the company, the manufacture and maintenance of sports equipment, grew to such a degree that it separated into an independent company that is still in existence today.

Marshall was responsible for the design and manufacture of the sports equipment for the then newly-built Northwood Stadium. However, Marshall decided to concentrate his effort on the core

*Top left: Founder George Dewey. **Above:** early production at the Old Mill circa 1956. **Left:** This picture shows a 'Rival' fitting made from bronze so the ladder could be used in munition factories. **Bottom left:** The Old Mill in Shelton. **Below:** A G.C. Dewey & Son exhibition at Bakewell carnival circa 1965.*

business activities of G. C. Dewey & Son Ltd, and the sports division was eventually sold.

G C Dewey & Son Ltd was by now employing ten full-time joiners and was predominantly producing ladders. Despite that  concentration on one primary product the firm still made furniture for Lewis's department store in Hanley (now Debenham's) and did all the general joinery for the Cope Stick & Farrell building that was to dominate Victoria Road for many years.

George, now past retirement age, moved to Rhyl then, Blackpool, where he started the Blackpool Ladder Centre that continued to survive under different ownership until 2010. The Blackpool venture was not out of the blue, as in  the early 1950s father and son would travel to Blackpool by train to meet the window cleaners of the area to produce bespoke ladders for them. Getting the orders was no ordeal, but delivering the finished goods however was an altogether more challenging matter in the 1950s.

Meanwhile, the day to day running of the company was now down to the full stewardship of Marshall Dewey. Under his control and guidance the business grasped modern production techniques and practices - both on the shop floor, and in the office where Marshall was ably assisted by Wendy, his wife.

In 1984 Neale Dewey joined the company. Today Neale is the firm's Managing Director. His wife Julie assists in the accounts office. Neale and Julie's sons Leigh, Scott and Ben help in production and warehousing.

Four generations of Dewey's have now worked for the company that still predominantly sells ladders - a product that its founder modestly described in the Evening Sentinel in 1966 as 'basic straightforward work'.

The company continues to flourish, being the only remaining ladder manufacturer and retailer in England north of Birmingham. It has fully encompassed the electronic age running three e-commerce sites, and has supplied its products throughout the UK for such diverse projects as the Channel Tunnel and the Docklands Light Railway. A far cry from the humble beginning at the 'Old Mill'.

Meanwhile, G C Dewey & Son Ltd remains a family-owned and run business, with Stoke-on-Trent at its heart.

Top left: *Degreasing baths circa 1970.* **Top right:** *Marshall and Wendy Dewey receiving a National Safety Award in 1976.* **Centre:** *Company vehicles from 1970 (top), 1977 (left) and 1980 (right).* **Left: and below:** *G.C. Dewey & Son Ltd's City Ladder Works, Victoria Road, Fenton.*

Diamond Interiors - A Four Generation Family Company

The Diamond Tile Company Limited in Hanley is unique. Diamond has been a family company for four generations. It has fought its way through four recessions and one world war, but still leads the way, having evolved into one of Britain's largest independent retail showrooms for bathrooms, kitchens, bedrooms and tiles.

The company was established in 1932 by Robert Harry Carden Cliff who was a potters' factor. He took over the run-down Diamond Pottery Company, which produced a variety of pottery items and china dolls, as payment for a debt.

Diamond was in a poor state: it had five bottle ovens, leaking roofs, and buildings that were about to collapse. 'Harry' Cliff tried to make the pottery firm profitable and began manufacturing ceramic tiles for fireplaces which were much in demand. Harry added a fireplace slabbing shop, in which he soon had 10 tile 'slabbers' manufacturing basic fireplaces and selling them all over the country.

In 1934, at the age of 14, Dorothy, Harry's daughter, joined her father to help in the office as a book keeper. Later Dorothy became Company Secretary, a position she kept for over 60 years.

Pre-war the company employed over a hundred people, making the firm one of the largest tile manufacturers in the area.

Tom Staton a pottery manager joined Diamond in 1941, he and Dorothy married in 1944, the day before he left to serve in the RAF. In the meantime the War Department took over Diamond's premises to store war supplies, including bales of hessian for camouflage which was used to cover Sheltons' iron and steel factory and warehouses that were prime targets for German bombers.

Dorothy remained at Diamond throughout the war keeping a record of what was delivered and what was collected.

During the war the local hospital asked Harry to manufacture dolls to give the children who were in hospital at Christmas.

Harry had the moulds made, and once they were fired his wife Florrie painted the faces. Dorothy helped to make the dolls' clothes and dress them. Doll production continued until it was stopped by the war department for using coloured glazes.

Tom returned from the war and due to the high demand for tiled fireplaces installed one of the first French Gottignie electric multi passage kilns, which could produce various shapes and sizes of tiles. In 1961 with the decline of tiled fireplace sales and the high costof the electricity Tom sold the kiln to H & R Johnsons tiles for their new factory in India.

Mr J. Lawton who was employed by Johnsons of Tunstall had the task of dismantling, numbering and packing each piece. He then went over to Bombay and rebuilt the kiln which continued to make tiles for many years.

Diamond replaced the Gottignie kiln with a more efficient gas kiln but stoped manufacturing tiles when it could not not be changed over to North Sea Gas.

In 1961 Tom Staton, now managing director, saw the future in the manufacture of modern fireplaces. He turned part of Diamond's warehouse into the first retail fireplace showroom in Stoke-on-Trent, replacing the thick bland fireplace tiles with colourful new materials such as marble, stone and slate.

Tom turned the 'fire frame' on its side so that the inside of the fire frame measured 20" wide x 16" high, and lifted it off the floor so it could have a raised hearth and plinth on which televisions could be placed. He patented the design and called it 'The Kingsley Patent 'Hole in the Wall' Fire'. It was a unique design and sold well, giving customers a wide choice of designs, including copper, brass or stainless steel frames and canopies all made by 'Kingsley' in their sheet metal and slabbing shops. Many of today's modern fireplaces are based on Tom's 'Hole in

the Wall' design. A few years later he designed Kingsley centre fires to add to the range, the only company whose centre fires could actually take both solid fuel or a log burning gas fire. Kingsley fires were sold throughout Britain and around the world.

Harry Cliff retired in 1967. Tom Staton was joined by his son John. Part of the fireplace showroom was extended and changed into the first retail showroom, displaying locally manufactured Twyfords and Armitage bathrooms in room settings tiled by Richards and Johnsons tiles.

In 1971 Tom's daughter Carol joined the firm to learn how to take over her mother's role of Secretary. But Carol did not like bookwork. Susan Adams, who started as an office junior in 1973, replaced Dorothy as Company Secretary in 1991.

Top left: A 2010 view of The Diamond Tile Company Ltd's showroom. Bottom left: Dorothy Staton and her husband Tom pictured in 1970. Above: The Kingsley Patent 'Hole in the Wall' design, CS 100. Below: An aerial view of the The Diamond Tile premises in 1972.

Dorothy remains as chairperson today, but stopped going into Diamond on a daily basis in 2004 at the age of 84, after 70 years service.

Tom began to expand the wall and floor tile side of the business in both retail and trade with the help of William (Bill) Bourne who was made a Director in 1972; he had worked for Diamond as a slabber since leaving school, and with his extensive tiling knowledge, managed Diamond's expanding tile-contracting division while John and Carol developed Diamonds tile distribution, supplying retail tile shops and trade tilling accounts.

In 1975, taking advantage of the ever increasing market for home improvement, a section of the showroom was redesigned showing quality English fitted kitchens from Hygena, English Rose, Elizabeth Ann, Easthams and Wrighton. When Wrighton's started to produce Bedroom furniture Diamond was one of the first showrooms to display the new ranges.

Not only did The Diamond/Kingsley group of companies supply the fireplace, bathroom, kitchen, bedroom and tiles for customers homes but was the only company in the area that if required could arranged the installation of the items which was unique at that time.

Sadly, Tom Staton passed away in 1985. His son John left Diamond in 1989, and Tom's daughter, Carol Staton, took over as Managing Director from her mother Dorothy in 1991. Carol already a successful business person was determined not only to make sure Diamond would continue to thrive but that the showrooms would be one of the largest and best in the UK. She sought out the finest products, not only from the remaining British manufacturers but also from Europe. With her knowledge of interior design Carol made sure that every display in Diamond's showroom was appealing to customers, both aesthetically and economically, showing customers how they could make their rooms look just like those shown in the leading home design magazines, but at affordable prices and if installation was required it was carried out with the minimum amount of stress and disruption.

Almost twenty years later Carol is very pleased to have a dedicated and loyal team working beside her. As well as Secertary Sue Adams who has been with her for 37 years, Mark, Carol's son, joined the company in 2001 and today is Diamond's Financial Director. Louise, Carol's Daughter, also joined the family company in 2005 after taking a degree in Business and Design at Manchester University. Louise is the Director in charge of Design and specializes in unique bathroom designs and wet room areas, her expertise has been acknowledged by a

leading bathroom design award and media articles. Bathroom Designer ranges available from Diamond include Villeroy and Boch, Jacuzzi, Kohler , Daryl, Aqata, Utopia and Ambiance Bain.

Nick Durber controls Diamond's Kitchen and Bedroom Department. He is an expert on kitchen and bedroom design continually impressing customers with his knowledge and products from manufactuers such as Wentworth and Nolte kitchen furniture, Miele, Neff, Boch, Siemens & Franke kitchen appliances and Hulsta, Nolte and Birch bedrooms.

Customers are able to view their newly-designed rooms on a large wall-mounted screen in the bathroom, kitchen and bedroom departments whilst enjoying a coffee or tea. Design changes can be made while the customer is watching so they have a superb view of what their room would look like before they leave the showrooms.

Carol continues to have a very active roll in the day to day actiivities of the Company, although still enjoying the selling of products and choosing the new ranges for display in the showroom she also oversees the in-house installation side of the company.

Paul Clowes, Diamonds General Manager who joined Diamond in 1998, now runs the extensive tile department. He has considerable product knowledge of each department and assists Carol in the day to day running of the Company.

Clients are invited to call at the Hanley showrooms and see for themselves why customers keep coming back, as well as recommending Diamond to their friends and neighbours. Diamond staff say "visit us as strangers, leave as friends".

Everyone cares passionately, not just about turning customers' ideas into reality, but to do so in a way which makes an often complex exercise thoroughly enjoyable and with the end result being a stunning room that they can enjoy for many years.

Carol Staton is very proud that Diamond is the largest and most prestigious 4th generation family-run company of its kind.

Diamond's unrivalled reputation was built by giving customers exactly what they require coupled with old-fashioned professional service; that ethos remains stronger than ever today.

Facing page: Examples of kitchen and bathrooms on view at The Diamond Interiors showroom. *Above:* Louise discusses bathroom design with customers. *Left:* Nick shows Paul and Sue his latest design with the help of a wall-mounted screen. *Below:* Three generations of the family still involved in the business today: Dorothy (centre), Carol (right) and Louise .

Bassett's of Tittensor - Five Generations of Road Transport

R.G. Bassett & Sons Ltd, based at Transport House, Tittensor, near Stoke, is a name which has been familiar to generations of local folk. Today Bassett's is a market leader in the provision of U.K. Road Haulage, Warehousing and Driver Training Services.

The story of Bassett's in transport began in 1897 with the founder of the firm, Joseph Bassett. Joseph lived and worked at Strongford Farm, between Trentham and Tittensor. He was a Victorian gentleman farmer who, inspired by the spirit of the age, saw relief from the drudgery of the land by letting steam power take the strain. But he went a step further than most, first becoming an agricultural contractor, and later a road builder.

From these early solid foundations the Company has, through vision, determination and the hard work of Joseph, his direct descendants Leonard John, Reginald (Reg) and the present Managing Directors, Leonard and Ashley Bassett, developed in to one of the region's leading providers of quality road haulage, warehousing and transport industry training services.

Transport services evolve in many ways, as do the customers to which their services relate. Towards the end of the twentieth century, the Company saw the demise of many of its established industrial and manufacturing partners which

Top: *In the mid-1920s Bassetts operated as a Petrol & Steam Haulage Contractor.* **Above left:** *Founder, Joseph Bassett.* **Above:** *A 1946 Bassett's Foden en route to Cadbury's at Bournville.*

it had been proud to serve for most of that era. Industries such as steel, tyres, pottery and mining were all significant contributors to both the local economy and Bassett's traffic portfolio. Regrettably those are now valued memories and reserved for the history books.

The intervening years have presented many opportunities and challenges in respect of all operational aspects of the family Company. Vehicle technology developed from a humble beginning using horses and carts to steam powered vehicles. Then petrol engines gave way to modern day diesel-engine lorries, which have capacities up to 480 brake horse power, operating to Euro 5 specification. This environmentally friendly equipment assists the delivery of consolidated part and full loads of up to 28 tonnes throughout Great Britain, either on a dedicated or spot-hire basis.

The majority of goods are transported by the Company's own dedicated modern fleet of 35 vehicles and 60 trailers which encompasses a comprehensive range of vehicle specifications to facilitate the wide-ranging service requirements of Bassett's extensive customer base.

Undoubtedly the strength of the Company has always been its ability, flexibility and sustained willingness to encompass change in every area of its operations. In order to offer clients the opportunity to deliver to all parts of the country on a next-day basis, Bassett's became a founder member-shareholder of Palletforce plc in 2001. The Company is one of the largest inputters of pallets into the Palletforce network which incorporates 90 members located nationwide and provides access to a combined fleet of over 4,000 vehicles.

In 2008 members of the fifth generation of the family, Claire and Laurence Bassett, were appointed as Directors of R.G. Bassett & Sons Ltd. They joined an experienced and innovative management team totally dedicated to the sustained provision of high standards of quality service at cost effective rates. Whilst current operations are focused around general road transport and its logistical parallels, Bassett's, over its long history, has successfully diversified into passenger transport (Bassett's Coachways Ltd: 1949-2003) and also moved into international haulage, having acquired the operating assets of Beresford Transport Ltd in 1996.

During the Company's long history, Bassett's has been proud and privileged to have employed many local people, who have greatly assisted in the provision of a professional service to both the traditional and emerging industries of North Staffordshire.

Today, still a family-run Company after more than a century in business, Bassett's looks forward to working with its valued clients across all industry sectors, to service their

transport requirements, and facilitate the progressive development of logistical partnerships to meet the challenges of the twenty first century.

Joseph Bassett, who founded the firm when Queen Victoria still reigned, would surely have been astonished and proud to see what his successors have achieved.

Top left: Reginald (Reg) Bassett who today's Company is named after. *Above:* Two of R.G. Bassett & Sons' modern fleet. *Left:* The current Directors of R.G. Bassett & Sons Ltd (from left to right): Ashley, Claire, Laurence and Leonard.

Portmeirion - A Design Legend

Portmeirion, on London Road, Stoke, was founded in 1960 by the legendary designer, Susan Williams-Ellis, and her husband Euan Cooper-Willis.

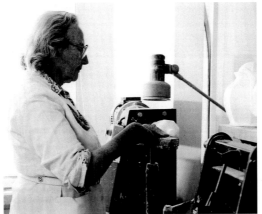

Susan was born in 1918 and was the daughter of Sir Clough Williams-Ellis, the architect and creator of Portmeirion Village in North Wales. Inheriting her father's love of design, Susan studied art and design under the tutelage of creative talents such as Bernard and David Leach, Henry Moore and Graham Sutherland. Keeping such interesting company, Susan's innate feel for shape, form and pattern inevitably flourished.

The opportunity to make full use of her design skills came along only when Susan's father asked her to create some ceramic gifts for the shop at Portmeirion Village.

By the late 1950s Susan's ceramic designs had become incredibly popular. So much so that in 1960 Susan and her husband Euan purchased A. E. Gray Ltd., a small pottery decorating company based in Stoke-on-Trent. This was followed by the acquisition of a second pottery company, Kirkhams Ltd., which could not only decorate pottery but also make it. This allowed Susan to design both shape and surface pattern which, in the 1960s, was unique. These two businesses were combined and Portmeirion Potteries was born. Portmeirion continues to manufacture some of Susan's designs in the same factory in Stoke-on-Trent to this day.

Malachite (1960) and Moss Agate (1961) were amongst Susan's earliest designs. Neither was produced in large quantities, but both received high critical acclaim. The iconic Totem design followed in 1963.

Totem, with layered glazes of various hues, brought Portmeirion to the forefront of fashion in an era of evolving and revolutionary British design. Bold, abstract, patterns of embossed spirals and stars, coupled with striking cylindrical drum-like shapes of coffee pots, cups and saucers, cream jugs and sugar bowls, resulted in a unique collection.

Susan created Magic City in 1966 and Magic Garden in 1970, both featuring strong, bold surface patterns. Many years later Susan's original prototype for Magic Garden was found in the cellar of Bank House (Susan and Euan's home that was attached to the factory). The design had been directly penciled onto a cylindrical coffee pot and was simply stunning – so much so that it inspired Portmeirion to create its Magic Garden Graphite collection in celebration of its 50th anniversary in 2010.

'Botanic Garden', Portmeirion's most-recognised design, was launched in 1972. The design was inspired by the discovery

Top: Founder, Susan Williams-Ellis. Left: A drawing of the Portmeirion bottle kilns. Above: Botanic Garden teapot.

Keele University also awarded Susan the Honorary Degree of Master of the University for an Outstanding Contribution to the Ceramics Industry Internationally.

Sadly, Susan Williams-Ellis passed away in November, 2007. But with nearly fifty years of creativity her heritage will last as long as ceramics. Her achievements place her firmly in the company of a small group of great 20th Century designers, whilst her belief that tableware should be both beautiful and practical, continues to permeate Portmeirion's design ethos.

Portmeirion remains at the forefront of innovative design. Its latest collections include the immensely popular 'Sophie Conran for Portmeirion' and the distinctive and instantly recognisable 'The Very Hungry Caterpillar' licensed collection.

In 2006, Portmeirion Potteries acquired Pimpernel, the premier brand for placemats and coasters, and in 2009 purchased the Spode and Royal Worcester brands. After this expansion, the company was renamed Portmeirion Group.

*Top left: Portmeirion's 'Totem' range from the archive. **Above right:** 'The Very Hungry Caterpillar' licensed collection. **Below:** The Sophie Conran for Portmeirion collection.*

of some antique botanical books. With a variety of individual floral decorations, Botanic Garden encapsulated a new mood for casual dining. It became an instant success and went on to become a classic of British ceramics, and one of the world's most popular floral tableware designs. The range continues to be made at Portmeirion's factory in Stoke-on-Trent.

Susan always intended her pottery designs to fit comfortably with everyday life. In her quest for success, and to achieve that objective, she was heavily involved in the manufacture of all her designs. Such involvement in both design and production was rare, and when combined with Susan's style and creativity, it was unique.

Susan received an honorary fellowship from University of Arts, London in 2005. At the time she said, "I decided to pursue pottery, rather than painting, mainly because I wanted to create affordable and beautiful things. Being in Stoke has been a wonderful part of my life. The people of Stoke are really the nicest people one could ever meet, and their hard work has established Portmeirion and enabled us to sell our pots around the world. I have been very fortunate."

Spode - A Formula for Success

Josiah Spode I (1733-1797) founded his Stoke-on-Trent based pottery company in 1770. His skill and dedication led to two major achievements that would redefine the pottery industry: the development of a superior formula for fine bone china, and the perfection of blue under-glaze printing.

Josiah began his career in the pottery industry at the age of 16. After working for many of the best potters in the Stoke-on-Trent area, including Thomas Whieldon, Josiah set up his own small pottery factory in 1760 and in 1770 established the Spode pottery company.

Purchasing land adjacent to the factory, Josiah was able to make full use of the canal system that now served Stoke-on-Trent, allowing raw materials to be brought in, and finished goods out to market.

In 1778, Josiah sent his son, Josiah II, to London to open a showroom and shop. This shrewd decision meant that Spode had direct information about the wealthy customer base in London. As a consequence Spode was able to design and manufacture items that customers actually wanted.

At that time Chinese porcelain, decorated in blue and white, was becoming increasingly difficult to obtain as imports slowed due to an auction ring that was lowering the profits of the Chinese exporters. In 1784, in response to this opportunity, Josiah developed a technique of transfer printing designs engraved on copper plates. The Willow collection was designed and manufactured, and in 1816 the iconic Blue Italian pattern was also introduced.

After much experimentation, Josiah and his son perfected the recipe for fine bone china – a formula that redefined the pottery industry.

Top: Founder, Josiah Spode. Left: Blue Italian is one of the collections that secured Spode's reputation as a leader in the ceramic industry. Below: Many items in Blue Italian are now being manufactured at Portmeirion Group's factory in Stoke-on-Trent.

When Josiah II himself died in 1827 he was buried with his father at St Peter's Church, in Stoke.

Josiah II's own second son, Josiah III (1777-1829), had been initiated into the pottery business by his grandfather. When Josiah III married Mary Williamson at the age of 38 he had retired from the business, but he returned 12 years later to run the company after his father's death.

Tragically Josiah III died suddenly at the family home just two years later.

The company was sold to W. T. Copeland and Garrett in 1833. It remained in the Copeland family until 1966.

Brilliant white and translucent, Spode's bone china inspired new designs and finishes. It was of superior quality and strong, whilst looking extremely delicate. The formula made the Spode name famous around the globe.

Josiah Spode died in 1797. On his father's death, Josiah II returned from London to run the Spode business in Stoke-on-Trent.

Dedicated to the local community, Josiah II built cottage homes for his factory workers in Penkhull, a village next to Stoke, where he also built his own home which he named The Mount. He also donated money towards the rebuilding of the church in Stoke where he was senior churchwarden.

During this time, ceramic slabs were laid at the cornerstones of the church which were inscribed "transmit to generations far remote invaluable memorials of the perfection to which the Potter's Art in the neighbourhood had arrived in the early 19th century".

In 2009 Portmeirion Group acquired the Spode brand. In its dedication to the development and success of Spode and its product range, Portmeirion Group have brought the manufacture of many items in Spode's iconic catalogue back to Stoke-on-Trent – a decision that has been welcomed by Spode's customers, collectors and the Stoke-on-Trent community alike. Now items in the classic Blue Italian collection and Woodland range can be seen progressing through at least 20 pairs of hands in Portmeirion Group's factory.

To reflect Spode's continued relevancy to contemporary design in the modern day environment, a new logo was developed in 2010 that embodies key characteristics of the original logo to reinforce Spode's strong historical roots.

Portmeirion Group is delighted to have become the custodian of this great British name, one which two centuries ago found the 'formula for success' and inspired a whole industry.

Top left and top left inset: Spode's Christmas Tree pitcher and plate. **Top right:** *A backstamp for Blue Italian with the new Spode logo and 'Made in England'.* **Left:** *Part of the Woodland range.*

Bailey, Wain and Curzon - Solicitors of Note in Fenton

The town of Fenton is located at the south side of the City of Stoke-on-Trent, bordered on the west by the River Trent and the Cockster Brook to the south and east. From Longton in the east to Stoke in the west the main roads now known as King Street and City Road follow the route of the old Roman road known as Rykeneld Street. It was here in 1953, only yards from the Roman crossroads (now Christchurch Street, Manor Street and City road), that Thomas Bailey set up his own legal practice. The practice would eventually evolve into today's well-known firm of Bailey, Wain and Curzon, now based in Springfield House in Baker Street.

Articled to Harold Grindey, a Stoke Solicitor, in November, 1940, Thomas Bailey passed his intermediate exams and then enlisted with the Royal Corps of Signals on 23 April, 1942. He resisted several attempts to have him promoted from Private and served with the Royal Scots on the front line, seeing service in North Africa, Sicily, Italy and Palestine. Demobbed in December, 1946, he returned to his Articles and was finally admitted as a Solicitor on 1 June, 1948. Tom Bailey worked initially with solicitors who had themselves been admitted in the previous century, Edward Burgess Sharpley, the Town Clerk of Stoke-on-Trent for 45 years, was admitted in 1900, and Reginald Challinor in 1890. Tom first opened an office in the northern town of Tunstall but soon returned to his roots in Fenton, purchasing a property on City Road.

Tom describes himself in those days as a "bread and butter lawyer" dealing mainly with clients involved in divorce, workmen's compensation and the Rent Acts. He was joined in 1960 by Edwin John Wain, a first class advocate who was soon prosecuting in the local courts for the Staffordshire Police; he remained in the partnership until 1984 when he was appointed

HM Coroner for the North Staffordshire District and he held that office for 19 years before retirement. John Wain has always been proud of the fact that in that time he was never appealed against. Another local solicitor joined the partnership in 1965 - Douglas Macmillan, leaving in 1973, after which Anthony Curzon arrived; shortly afterwards the firm changed its title to the present name.

Robert Bailey, Tom Bailey's son, transferred his Articles from a Manchester firm to his father in 1975 and became a partner shortly afterwards, later being joined by David Moore in 1978.

By this time the firm had diversified, now being heavily involved in prosecution and defence work, along with a

Top left: Founder, Thomas Bailey. *Top right:* The original premises in City Road, Fenton. *Left:* Old (left) and modern (above) views of Fenton Town Hall. Note the spire in the old picture which was removed sometime later as it was deemed unsafe.

Anthony Curzon meanwhile has maintained the connection with the local Coronership, having been Deputy for more than 25 years. He is a past President of both the North Staffordshire Law Society and the West Midlands and Central Wales Coroners' Society. David Moore has been a Deputy District Judge for many years.

Increasing workloads have led to departmentalisation. Principally private client work, the firm no longer deals with

thriving conveyancing and probate practice, David Moore concentrating on divorce and employment law.

By 1978 the firm had outgrown the offices in City Road and had bought premises adjacent to Fenton Town Hall in Baker Street, named after William Meath Baker, who had paid for the Hall in 1889 as the new centre of Fenton. The square in Fenton is a gathering place for many locals and has impressive buildings on two other sides, Bank Buildings to the north and Christ Church to the south.

In 1984, shortly after John Wain's appointment as Coroner, Tom Bailey retired from the partnership to become a consultant, a role he continues to perform, still regularly attending at the office twice a day.

criminal matters but concentrates on Conveyancing; Probate Wills, Trusts and Powers of Attorney/Court of Protection; Divorce Matrimonial and Employment Law; Personal Injury Claims, Contract and Professional Negligence.

The firm prides itself on the loyalty of its clients and that over 60 years the sons and daughters and grandchildren of many of Tom Bailey's early clients, as well as more recent ones, still appreciate the personal attention which the partners offer, and the help of dedicated staff, most of whom have been with the firm for very many years.

Top Left: *The partners in 1978. From L-R: David Moore, Robert Bailey, Tom Bailey, John Wain and Anthony Curzon.*
Top right: *Partners and staff pose for a picture in 1978.*
Left: *Christ Church, Fento, built by Charles Lynam in 1890-91. The tower followed in 1899 in a Gothic revival style.*
Above: *Today's partners, L-R: Robert Bailey, David Moore and Anthony Curzon.*

S Keeling & Co. - Prospering Through Work

Timber merchants S. Keeling & Co. Ltd have been based in Etruria since 1974, but the firm has a far longer history. Thomas Keeling, the founder of the Keeling dynasty, embarked on several business ventures, including buying the Queens Hotel in Hanley. Unfortunately it failed when a new railway line that was expected to bring customers missed the site by miles.

The hotel was sold to the Corporation at a considerable loss. The premises, however, renamed the Victoria Hall, became the town hall. Thomas Keeling's initials can still be seen on the Bagnall Street side of the building.

Thomas Keeling now bought an island off Vancouver in British Columbia, Canada. He took two of his sons with him, but left behind his wife, another son, Sam, and a daughter.

Sam Keeling and his mother invested in a timber selling firm. That timber business, based in Copeland Street, Stoke, was inherited by Sam's son Geoffrey, and in turn by his son, another Sam. It flourished in Copeland Street until the Queensway motorway was planned. A necessary move was made to the firm's present location in Forge Lane, Etruria - a site which when first acquired was a compete wilderness.

Geoffrey Keeling's grandson David joined the firm in 1973.

In Forge Lane the timber firm became heavily mechanised, the staff, however, remained familiar faces; the majority started with Keeling's at the age of 16 and stayed through to retirement at 65.

By the mid-1980s the firm had three huge storage sheds containing timber from all over the world. Spruce and plywood came from Canada, but the best timber came from Russia.

For the future the plan is to continue to build on the firm's hard earned reputation – living up to the Keeling family motto: 'Floret qui laborat' – he who works prospers.

"I see our company continuing to consolidate its position locally as a reputable and reliable timber merchant" says Managing Director David Keeling, "We have an ongoing programme of modernisation to improve our sawmill, timber treatment plant and distribution service so that customers will benefit."

"Environmental issues continue to dominate our source of supply, and these markets are studied closely during political, civil and climatic change."

Top: *Sam Keeling and family.* ***Left:*** *The original building in Copeland Street which was home to the buisness until 1973.* ***Above:*** *Managing Director David Keeling and father Sam Keeling pictured in 2010.*

The Hanley - Building for the Future

From humble beginnings the Hanley Economic Building Society, based at Granville House, Festival Park, Hanley, has grown into an organisation which thousands of families and individuals rely upon.

With a network of Branches and Agencies located throughout North Staffordshire the Society combines the traditions of a mature organisation with the verve and efficiency of a modern business, with high-quality customer service at its core.

It was in 1854 that Earl Granville, Foreign Secretary in the Gladstone Government, and principal of the Shelton iron and steel works, founded the Society with the aim of fostering thrift amongst his employees and those living locally. What was then the Staffordshire Potteries Economic Permanent Building Society held its first meeting on 23 October, 1854 at Market Terrace, Hanley. The word 'permanent' in the name distinguished the Hanley from other early building societies which would be wound up once all their limited number of members had paid off their mortgages.

of a 56-year long career, the last 23 years of which would be as Managing Director.

By its centenary year in 1954 'the Hanley' could boast 8,000 members with assets of over £3 million.

Granville House, the Society's purpose-built head office at Festival Park, opened in 2009 having moved from its former Festival Park site it opened in 1992. By its 155th anniversary in 2009 it had grown to an organisation with 40,000 members, assets of £350 million, and was helping 6,000 customers to buy their own homes.

Today the Hanley is the most modern of financial institutions. Yet happily it is also one imbued with traditional values - which have enabled it to thrive in difficult times, and to continue providing an unrivalled quality of service.

Top left: Founder, Earl Granville. *Above:* Albion House, the original site of the Cheapside offices. *Left:* The Society's premises in the 1950s. *Below:* Granville House, the Society's purpose-built head office at Festival Park, which opened in 2009.

The Hanley began its life with assets of just £629. The first loan was for £75, to be repaid over 60 years. A name change came in 1930 – what now became the familiar Hanley Economic Building Society by then had assets of £340,000. A new head office was opened at 42 Cheapside, Hanley in 1935. By that time Mr W Rees Jones was the Society's Managing Director. W Rees Jones had started work for the Society in 1892, the beginning

Goodwins - The Golden Touch

The business was established by Charles Edwin Henry Goodwin in the 19th century. Charles came from a family of jewellers. He learnt the trade in his father's shop in Manchester, back in the days when shops stayed open until 10pm on Saturdays. Father and son specialised in clock and watch making, while the sale of wedding rings formed the most important part of the retail business.

In 1874 Charles Edwin moved to the Potteries and started his own business at 12 Hope Street, Hanley. In due course his own son, Charles Percival Morgan Goodwin, joined the firm, and when number 16 Hope Street became available, Charles Percival bought it. Operating as jeweller and watchmaker from the two premises, the business continued to grow, serving the needs of its customers even in troubled times during the two world wars when there was a real shortage of gold. Often long queues would form outside the shop in the hopes of being able to secure one of the few wedding rings available.

Goodwins the Jewellers has been part of Hanley since Victorian times. Today the family business combines the traditional craft skills of jewellery making with the ability to create designs to suit every occasion. Some readers may be fortunate enough to own a set of the 'Cup-Links' which the company manufactured to commemorate Stoke City FC's victory in the 1972 League Cup Final. In 2002 the business received the ultimate honour when it was chosen to manufacture a brooch which was presented to her Majesty Queen Elizabeth II, as part of her Golden Jubilee celebrations. A competition was run giving people the chance to create a design for the brooch. The winning design came from Mrs. Sally Tsang and the brooch was manufactured on the premises at Goodwins from gold donated by the local community.

Having taken it over in 1912 and been responsible for establishing and expanding the business, Charles Percival handed it down to the third generation of the family in 1959.

As before, the new generation continued the success and expansion of Goodwins. Charles David Goodwin was interested in jewellery manufacture and before long he seized the opportunity to acquire numbers 14 and 16a Hope

Top left: *Founder, Mr C E H Goodwin, outside his shop at 12, Hope Street, Hanley, circa 1900.* ***Left:*** *Mr C E H Goodwin, seated, is pictured with his family in 1916, Mr C P M Goodwin is standing behind.* ***Above:*** *An exhibition stand at Earls Court.*

manufacturing process is carried out on the premises, from the initial casting through to the setting of diamonds and other precious stones. Jewellery is still made in a very traditional manner and although some of the equipment has been modernised, many of the tools have not changed since Great Grandfather Charles Edwin Henry Goodwin's day and it is still the unique skills of the goldsmith which ensure the quality of the finished item.

Goodwins makes its own distinctive range of contemporary jewellery and supplies jewellers throughout the country with a range of Victorian reproduction jewellery. Expert repairs are also carried out in the workshop and customers often design their own unique pieces and have them manufactured on the premises.

Goodwins prides itself on its long-held reputation for value and delivering a first class service. The dedicated and knowledgeable staff have many years experience in helping couples choose the perfect rings and gifts for their special events.

As one of the Potteries longest established businesses, with long-serving, expert and friendly staff, Goodwins aim in the 21st century is to maintain and enhance the traditions and reputation established by previous generations and to continue to bring first class service and beautiful jewellery to the local community.

Street and make the premises into one. This was an event of some significance, resulting as it did in delivering pleasant, spacious premises with room to expand the manufacturing element even further. Numbers 12-16 Hope Street have remained the home of Goodwins Jewellers ever since.

Although the shop is situated just outside the main retail centre of the town, trade has never suffered and the great advantage of the Hope Street premises is that jewellery can be manufactured in the workshops above the retail shop - something that jewellers in a prime High Street location are not able to do.

In the early 1980s Charles David Goodwin's two children entered the business - Susan in 1983, and her brother Charles Phillip Mark the following year. The three of them worked together for some 15 years, with Charles Phillip practising as a goldsmith and Susan working in the office and shop. Charles David retired in 1997, and sadly both he and Charles Phillip died the following year, leaving Goodwins in the hands of Susan Goodwin and her mother, Mavis.

Goodwins manufacturing business is known in trade circles as G & S Jewellery and has been a regular exhibitor at major events, such as the annual Earls Court trade show in London. The entire

Top left: Sue Goodwin, Charles David Goodwin and Charles Philip Goodwin pictured on the occasion of Charles David's retirement in 1997. Top right: With experienced goldsmiths on site the team at Goodwins can source, design and create fine jewellery to specific requirements. Centre: The Golden Jubilee 2002 brooch manufactured by the company. Left: Goodwins, 2010 - the business continues to thrive into the 21st century.

Steelite International - A Passion to Inspire

Steelite International is a world-leading manufacturer of award-winning chinaware for the international hospitality industry. The company's products are manufactured at its Dalehall factory in Stoke-on-Trent – one of the most modern production facilities in the world.

Though the present company was formally established only in 1983 its antecedents go back much further. Today the company exports to over 120 countries.

Dunn Bennett & Co was founded over a century ago by master potter William Dunn and Thomas Wood Bennett, a gifted salesman.

In 1911 the company equipped Scott's expedition to the South Pole - free of charge - in return for being able to advertise its tableware as being remarkably durable and tough.

The Dalehall works was acquired in 1937.

'Steelite' vitreous body was created in 1968. That same year Dunn Bennett & Co Ltd was acquired by Doulton & Co and became its Hotelware Division.

In 1983 David Edward Dunn Johnson bought the hotelware division from Royal Doulton and formed Steelite International. The following year Steelite International Australia was established, the first of several overseas subsidiaries. Expansion followed. By the mid-1980s sales doubled to over £17 million. In 1989 the first phase of manufacturing renovation was completed, with 8,000mÇ of space dedicated to decorating and glazing. The new Decorating and Glazing Department was officially opened by HRH the Princess Margaret.

In 1993 a second phase of renovation was completed. Another 8,000mÇ of space was dedicated to clay making and biscuit firing. With total investment on first and second phase amounting to some £12million the factory could now produce 350,000 pieces every week. By the following year export sales alone amounted to £10 million. A third phase of development was completed in 1997. This increased overall capacity to 450, 000 pieces per week at a cost of a further £5m.

David Johnson sold the company in 2002. More investment soon followed, increasing capacity to half a million pieces per week.

In January, 2006, came a new management buyout led by Chief Executive, Kevin G Oakes. The new team also included Richard Poole, Finance Director, Bernard

*Top left: Dalehall Works entrance in 1992. **Left and below:** Two views inside the Sliphouse in 1984. **Above:** An old company brochure featuring Steelite's Marina Red Empire range.*

Matthews, Production Director and John Miles, President Steelite International USA.

A Stock Market flotation was soon launched.

By the end of 2006, company turnover was £48.2 million, with exports accounting for 72% of sales.

In 2007 Steelite won top awards in The Sentinel Business Awards: Business of the Year and Design Excellence. The Float range won the Pencil Award at the Design & Art Direction ceremony.

Heath's Filtration building was now renovated. This once fine Georgian property was originally built as the vicarage to St. Paul's. Throughout the 20th century it was owned by the Heath's company and had numerous structural additions made through the 1970s.

Steelite International had acquired the Heath's site in 1988 with a view to incorporating the building into its manufacturing area. When the factory extension was built in 2002, however, it was found to be not needed. The building was unused but fell within the conservation area. The City Council's Directorate of Regeneration and Community facilitated the renovation via the Middleport Townscape Heritage Initiative. Steelite International was particularly grateful to its funding partners.

Meanwhile, new products were developed apace. In February, 2008, Symmetry, Spyro and Z were launched. Overseas initiatives also increased, with Stuart Wilkinson being appointed as Steelite International's presence in the United Arab Emirates.

The company celebrated its 25th anniversary looking forward to a prosperous future. The global recession, however, soon dampened expectations. In 2009 redundancies came as an unwelcome consequence of the worldwide recession alongside short-time working. Product innovation however, continued. Low temperature glazing was introduced. Awards too continued to be gained, whilst a new Head of Marketing and Design – Chris Proud - was appointed along with a vice president for European Sales – Simon Treanor. The Marketing department was brought back in-house in 2010 as a new range of buffet items – Roselli Risers and Canyon Chafers – was launched.

Also newly launched was a Lifetime Edge Chip Warranty on Distinction & Performance ranges, extending the company's commitment to quality. A comprehensive range of the company's products can be seen on their website at www.steelite.com.

After two years of recession the company was now able to start recruiting factory staff once again.

Today the company with 'a passion to inspire' employs over 750 people and has an annual turnover of £50 million.

Top left and below: Views of the Steelite International plc, Orme Street, Stoke-on-Trent, premises. Top right: Kevin G Oakes, Chief Executive. Centre: Mix it up with Taste, a range that adds style to casual dining (left) and part of Steelite's Organics collection (right).

E A Heath (R&W) Ltd - From Scrap to Art

Still a family firm after more than half a century in business, the name of E A Heath (R&W) Ltd based on the Fenpark Industrial Estate, in Park Lane, Fenton, has become well known for much more than just recycling scrap metal.

Mr Edward Heath Senior founded the recycling business in the 1950s, collecting rags and woollens whilst working at the Royal Cinema in Sanford Hill. His boss had paid him £5 holiday pay with which he started his firm. With the holiday money Edward invested in some 'swag' - things such as exercise books, pencils or toys that could be exchanged with members of the public for bags of old clothing.

Not for Edward the traditional horse and cart however, even then he had more up to date transport, albeit only an old Morris Cowley, in which he went out in to do his collecting.

As the business improved a friend helped out, and eventually Edward was able to buy a Morris PB van to replace the old Cowley.

With expansion two people were employed and a second vehicle acquired. With that growth the fledgling firm moved first to business premises in Sandford Hill, which was in a farm yard. As the business grew even more a move was made to premises in Hartshill, increasing the staff to eight.

In 1960, after three years at Hartshill, the business moved again, this time to premises in Park Lane, Fenton. With the move came a change of business status - to a limited company and at the same time Edward and Joan adopted a baby girl named Sandra.

By now the firm was employing 24 staff who sorted rags and woollens into various grades of cloth, roofing rags and industrial wiping rags. In the upstairs of the premises women sorted woollens into 78 grades of colours and textures. There were also five men who were employed as strippers! They took off all the buttons, linings etc. from clothes to leave just the cloth material.

The business remained located in the Park Lane premises for 11 years but these were demolished in 1971. As a consequence the firm moved to its present location on the Fenpark Industrial Estate.

Top left: Mr & Mrs Joan and Edward "Ted" Heath, pictured in 1946. *Top right:* Staff take a well-earned break to pose for a photograph in the 1960s. *Left:* A Heath company vehicle outside their premises in Fenpark, Fenton. *Above:* Loading up after sorting and bailing rags and woollens.

By the mid-1980s the introduction of nylon and synthetic fibres had significantly affected the mills since a large proportion of materials could not be recycled. However, as most of the Heath's staff were nearing retirement age the company took the decision to give up the rag and woollens business and instead concentrate on the recycling of non-ferrous metals, an activity which today still forms the core of the business.

Edward Heath Senior died in 1980, but the traditional family business carried on with Mrs. Joan Heath as Managing Director and Edward 'Eddie' Heath jnr as Director.

Mrs. Heath, who is known affectionately to locals as "Ma" Heath, has outside interests which include playing cribbage, completing crosswords and going to horse shows with her granddaughter who competes in eventing (dressage, show jumping and cross country). At the age of 65 she wanted to learn how to fly so had flying lessons even though she has a fear of heights.

The founder's son, Eddie Heath's interests include playing darts, skiing and scuba diving as well as receiving national fame for constructing specialist bonfires to raise money for the Air Ambulance. Eddie, a former Stafford College of Art student, has become something of a local legend as a result of setting fire to several famous buildings. Not the originals, we hasten to add, but remarkably accurate replicas built from unwanted wooden pallets.

It started in 1992 with a couple of battleships and since then has taken in flaming images of The White House, Houses of Parliament, The Tower of London, Big Ben, Wembley's Twin Towers, Dracula's Castle, a 30-foot galleon, the head of a T-Rex, and even an exact replica of his local village pub, The Royal Oak (including dartboard), and many more at which this biennial spectacle has unfolded. His main aim is raising vital funds for charities such as the Air Ambulance and Cheadle Hospital. The events have raised tens of thousands of pounds and customers at the yard have also contributed generously to the cause by donating unwanted ferrous scrap metal which is weighed in and the proceeds given to the Air Ambulance fund.

Meanwhile, Eddie's burning ambition has given delight to thousands, and turned scrap into genuine works of art.

Top: Eddie Heath infront of the remarkable replica of the White House which he built with old wooden pallets. Inset shows it alight on bonfire night as part of a fund raising event for the Air Ambulance. Left: Joan about to set off for the skies. Above right: Mrs. Joan Heath, 2010.

Ferro - Superior Materials

Ferro Corporation is a leading global supplier of technology-based materials for a broad range of manufacturers. Its materials enhance the performance of products in electronics, solar energy, telecommunications, appliances, automotive, household furnishings, building and renovation, pharmaceuticals, and industrial markets. The firm's corporate vision as a company is 'to enhance life through superior materials performance'.

11 October, 2009, marked the 90th anniversary of the founding of Ferro as the Ferro Enamelling Company, in Cleveland, Ohio, in the USA. Employees across the world celebrated their company's rich and diverse history, not least Ferro's British employees.

Ferro (Great Britain) Limited, based in Nile Street, Burslem, Stoke-on-Trent, is a subsidiary of Ferro Corporation, itself still based in Cleveland, USA. The English arm of this global company was first incorporated on 28 December, 1929, as The Ferro Enamelling Company (Eng) Ltd. The business can however, rightly claim to now have local roots in Burslem which go back to 1922.

The Ferro Enamelling Company in England was originally based at Wombourne, near to Wolverhampton, and was at the forefront in the early developments of vitreous enamel coatings. In 1974, Ferro acquired the business of James Davies (Burslem) Ltd in order to establish a local presence in the heart of the pottery industry.

The present Nile Street site was originally purchased by James Davies in 1934 and it has been in continuous operation ever since; it is now the registered office of Ferro (Great Britain) Limited.

James Davies originally founded his ceramic transfer business in 1922, calcining his own colours and fluxes. When he first moved on to the Nile Street site in 1934 frits and fluxes were produced on coal-fired smelters before being converted to oil, town gas and finally North Sea Gas in 1969. The last member of the Davies family to be associated with the business was Mrs. Isabel Poole, the daughter of James Davies; she took over the day to day running of the company in 1946 due to her father's ill-health.

Frit and pigment manufacturing was transferred to the Wombourne site in 1984 before eventually being transferred in 1993 to other European manufacturing sites. Glaze manufacturing however, which commenced in 1934, continues in Burslem to this day.

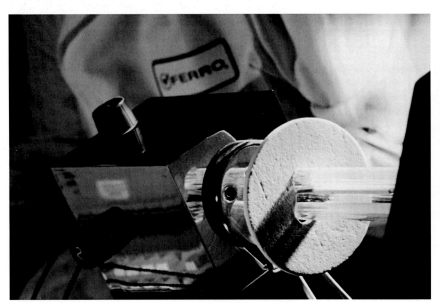

Top: *Glaze Milling.* ***Left:*** *Quality Control.*
Above: *Decoration Colour Process.*

Over the course of the 20th century and into the 21st many improvements have been made. The site was almost completely rebuilt during the late 1990s.

But how did this globe spanning corporation begin?

It was back in 1919, with a total investment of just $1,000, that Harry D. Cushman first incorporated the Ferro Enamelling Company. The business produced porcelain enamel frit in a plant at East 56th Street in Cleveland. Frit is a complex glass that is a core ingredient in porcelain enamel.

Eight years later Ferro sets up a sales and service operation in Canada, marking the first porcelain enamel supply house in that country and the first step in building Ferro's extensive international network. By the end of the 1920s Ferro Canada was manufacturing – 'smelting' - frit in its own facility, a typical pattern for Ferro's international growth.

Ferro not only began sales and service operations in England in 1929 but that same year also built a manufacturing facility in Holland. Despite the Wall Street Crash the Ferro Enamelling Company chose this year to go public, obtaining its first listing on the American Stock Exchange.

In 1920 another business, the Ferro Enamel & Supply Company, was established by Robert A Weaver, expressly to market products manufactured by Harry Cushman's Ferro Enamelling Company.

Ferro Enamelling Company and Ferro Enamel & Supply Company merged in 1930 to form Ferro Enamel Corporation.

Faced with little fuel and a shortage of raw materials during the Second World War Ferro France created an innovative electric smelting method for producing frit which after the war Ferro was able to expand to other facilities.

Today, Ferro (Great Britain) Limited is a major supplier of frits, glazes, pigments, decorative enamels and speciality coatings across a wide range of industries and its products are exported to customers worldwide.

Today Ferro Corporation employs around 5,200 people worldwide with operations in 23 countries. 2009 recorded sales reached $1.7 billion.

Above: Quality Control Testing. *Below:* Ferro (Great Britain) Limited's Nile Street, Burslem, premises.

Johnson Tiles - A Century of Quality

With over 100 years' experience, Johnson Tiles is the United Kingdom's leading manufacturer and importer of ceramic wall and floor tiles. The company produces wall and floor tiles in Stoke-on-Trent to the highest of standards. Johnson's excellence in quality and design is recognised throughout the industry, not only in Britain, but across the globe. The experienced team based in Stoke-on-Trent travels the world to its sister ceramic tile manufacturing companies abroad, and to the rest of the world's ceramic industry to select the imported product portfolio which complements the company's own product range.

Ceramic tiles have been used for centuries. There is archaeological evidence that the use of wall and floor tiles in buildings existed in Egypt as long ago as 4,000 BC. By 900 AD the use of decorative tiles had become widely used in Persia, Syria and Turkey.

At the end of the 12th Century, as transportation and communication developed throughout the world, the use and manufacture of tiles spread across Europe. They were used mainly in churches and cathedrals to decorate the floors.

It was during the 18th Century that tiles were imported into Britain, so providing the initiative to develop the tile industry in this country. From early beginnings in Lambeth, Fulham, Bristol and Liverpool the industry developed in Staffordshire where there was already a thriving ceramics industry producing tableware.

During the Victorian era, tile companies began to patent their processes and the industry we know today was formed. At the beginning of the 20th Century it was said that no home, public building, hotel or institution was complete without ceramic tiles.

By 1918 the industry was producing more than a million square yards per year. The demand at that time was mainly for plain ceramic floor and wall tiling, and the craft of making specialist 'encaustic' floor tiles, originally used in cathedrals and churches, died out in all but a few manufacturers. In the 1920s ceramic tiles for fireplaces were developed, and this soon became an important part of the ceramic tile industry.

With typically up to four fireplaces in every home, this was a boom time for those involved in fireplace tile production. Even the recession of the 1930s saw very little effect on the profitability of the ceramic tile industry.

*Top: HRH the Prince of Wales pays a keen interest on his visit to the factory in 1913. **Left:** Tile inspection at Highgate in 1924. **Above:** An aerial view of Highgate Tile Works in the early 1960s.*

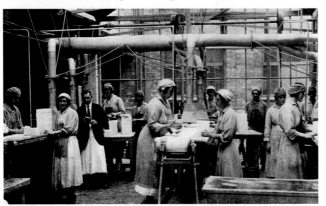

During the Second World War however, many companies were closed, and it was a very different industry which re-emerged at the war's end. Nothing would be the same again.

After the war, demand for perfect quality, sizing and shading caused manufacturers to incorporate more mechanisation into the way the tiles were manufactured. This was the prelude to the hi-tech industry which exists today.

The market place in the 1950s and 1960s demanded perfect quality, perfect sizing and perfect shading. During this period two companies had dominated Britain's tile industry, H & R Johnson Ltd - founded in 1901 - and Richards Tiles Ltd, founded in 1893.

Gradually, these two took over the smaller companies, and in 1968 then merged themselves. Between them the well-known names of Minton Hollins, T & R Boote, Maw, Malkin Edge, Sherwin & Cotton and Campbell Tiles were now interwoven into the structure of a single new company.

H & R Johnson-Richard Tiles Ltd (later H & R Johnson Tiles Ltd.), with its overseas companies on five continents, now became one of the largest manufacturers of ceramic tiles in the world.

During the 1970s the tile market in the UK developed into home improvement and DIY. It was a boom period for the industry, with H & R Johnson products leading the way and accounting for as much as 65% of all sales. Use of tiles in Britain doubled from 12 million square metres in 1970, and by 1991 had reached 38 million square metres.

Today's products are mostly mass produced, to extremely high standards of design and quality. Ceramic tiling on walls and floors is accepted as vital to the well decorated home, and in industrial situations where cleanliness and hygiene are essential.

Johnson Tiles, as the company is now known is a division of Norcros Group (Holdings) Limited, continues to lead the industry with a still-developing market stimulating even greater improvements in design, manufacturing, packaging and marketing.

Top left: Inkjet printing of tiles. *Bottom left:* A roller hearth tile kiln. *Above:* Body preparation area. *Below:* Johnson Tiles, Harewood Street, Tunstall, by night.

ACKNOWLEDGMENTS

The publishers would like to sincerely thank a number of individuals and organisations for their help and contribution to this publication.

This book would have been almost impossible without the kind co-operation of the following:

The Potteries Museum & Art Gallery

Borough Museum & Art Gallery, Newcastle under Lyme

The Warrillow Collection, Keele University Library

Steve Birks

William Blake

Getty Images

Speedway images courtesy of www.newcastlespeedwayhistory.co.uk